From Your Friends At The MAILBOX®

Back-To-School Book

GRADES 4–6

Editor In Chief:
Marge Michel

Product Director:
Kathy Wolf

Senior Editor:
Thad H. McLaurin

Editors:
Peggy W. Hambright, Elizabeth H. Lindsay,
Debra Liverman, Stephanie Willett-Smith

Copy Editors:
Debbie Blaylock, Lynn Bemer Coble, Jennifer Rudisill,
Debbie Shoffner, Gina Sutphin

Artists:
Jennifer Tipton Bennett, Cathy Spangler Bruce, Pam Crane, Clevell Harris,
Susan Hodnett, Sheila Krill, Rebecca Saunders, Donna K. Teal

Typographers:
Scott Lyons, Lynette Maxwell

Cover Artist:
Jennifer Tipton Bennett

Back-To-School Book

From Your Friends At *The Mailbox*®

Grades 4–6

About This Book

Look between these covers to find everything you need to make your back-to-school experience a success! We've included all-new ideas to help you get ready for the first day, organize your materials, and create eye-catching bulletin boards. We've selected teacher-tested open house ideas, technology tips, back-to-school literature suggestions, and much more for the intermediate classroom. The ideas in this book are arranged so that you can refer to a topic quickly and choose the ideas suited to your individual needs. We hope our *Back-To-School Book* gets your school year off to a great start!

Table Of Contents

Getting Acquainted 4

Classroom Management 14

Bulletin Boards 22

Open House Activities 30

Parent Communication 36

Positive Discipline 42

Student Motivation 46

Student Organization 52

Art Projects 56

Games 60

Writing 64

Technology 68

Literature 72

Charts And Forms 76

Reproducibles 81

Getting Acquainted

Here's The Scoop

Get the scoop on your students' summer vacations with this fun activity and display. On the first day of school, distribute one copy of the reproducible on page 81 to each student. Tell each student to write his name in the top scoop of each ice-cream cone. Next instruct him to read the category on each ice-cream cone, then write the name of one person, place, or thing that fits the category in each remaining ice-cream scoop. Tell students to lightly color each ice-cream cone and cut it out. Collect the cones and post each student's cone from the "Favorite Places Visited" category on a bulletin board titled "Here's The Scoop On Our Summer Vacations." After a few days, remove the cones from the display and post each student's cone from one of the other five categories. Continue changing ice-cream cones until each category has been displayed. Students will enjoy learning about their new classmates, and you'll have a hassle-free bulletin board for weeks!

Colleen Dabney—Gr. 6
Williamsburg Christian Academy
Williamsburg, VA

Team T's

This "T-rific" activity will build unity and camaraderie in your classroom. Ask each student to bring a plain, solid-colored T-shirt to school. As a class, brainstorm ideas for a class logo. List the ideas on the board and have your class vote for one idea. Then have each student use puff paints or fabric crayons to create the new class logo on his T-shirt. Encourage your class to proudly wear these T-shirts at school assemblies, at special school functions, and on field trips. What a great way to develop school pride and a sense of belonging!

Julie Eick-Granchelli—Gr. 4
Towne Elementary
Medina, NY

Lollipop Partners

Sweeten your students' first day with this tasty icebreaker. Purchase a bag of lollipops; then sort the lollipops into pairs according to their flavors. Hand each child one lollipop as he enters your room on the first day of school. Tell him not to eat it just yet. After all students have arrived, instruct each student to find another person in the class who has the same-flavor lollipop as him. Once all matches have been found, give students ten minutes to tell their partners about themselves. When the time is up, have each student introduce his partner to the class. After all the introductions have been made, let students eat their lollipops.

Patricia Altman—Gr. 6
Lewis M. Klein Middle School
Harrison, NY

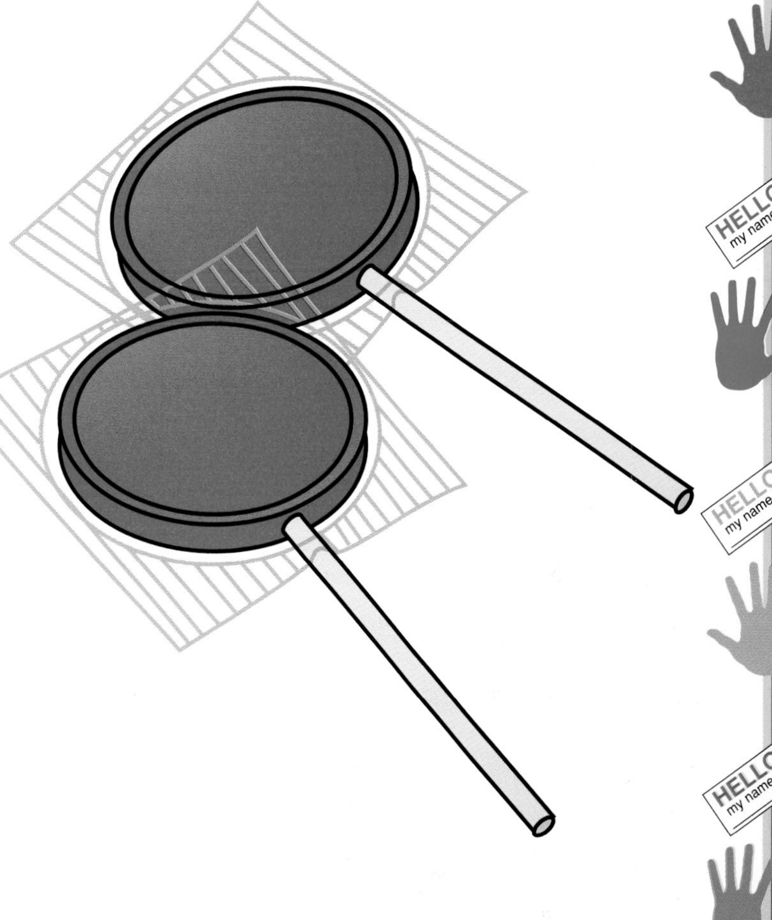

Hey, We're Neighbors!

Here is a fun way for students to get to know where their classmates live. Write your school's address on a school-shaped cutout; then post it in the center of a bulletin board titled "Home Sweet Home." Next give each student a house-shaped cutout and instruct him to write his home address on it. Use a local map to help you post each student's cutout on the bulletin board around the school cutout. Students will enjoy getting to know their neighbors.

Julie Eick-Granchelli—Gr. 4
Towne Elementary
Medina, NY

Laying The Foundation

Build a strong foundation for a new school year with this unique display. Cut out 20 cinder-block shapes from different-colored construction paper. On each cutout write a different sentence such as "I just moved here," "I like to draw," or "I have a pet." Circulate all the cinder-block cutouts throughout the room. Instruct each student to sign his name on every block that pertains to him. After each student has written his signature on the appropriate blocks, use the cutouts to build a wall on a bulletin board titled "Laying The Foundation For A New Year." Invite students to visit the display during their free time. Students will get to know others with whom they share similar interests and will start building friendships!

Julia Alarie—Gr. 6
Essex Middle School
Essex, VT

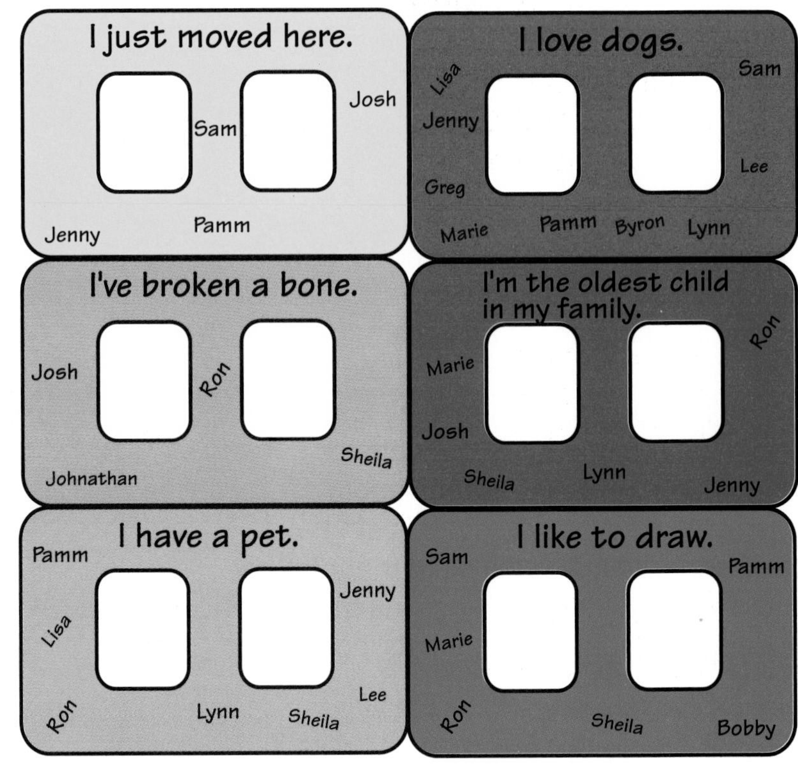

I got a letter from my teacher!

First-Day Letters

Get to know your students both personally and academically with this insightful homework assignment! Write a letter to your students, sharing some personal information about yourself such as hobbies and interests, where you have lived, your family, and how long you have been teaching. End the letter by assigning each student to write you a letter in return. Tell him the letter needs to include three paragraphs—one on family, one on hobbies and interests, and one on his favorite foods or sport. Distribute a copy of your letter to each student on the first day of school. Then explain to each student that the letter reveals his first homework assignment. Use the return letters to assess each student's writing skills and to learn more about each child's personality.

Lori Brandman—Gr. 5
Shallowford Falls Elementary
Marietta, GA

Wall Of Fame

Have students share information about themselves on a "Classroom Wall Of Fame!" Ask each student to bring in a small photograph of himself. Then give each child a 12" x 18" sheet of construction paper and have him divide the paper into eight sections as shown. Instruct students to label the eight sections: Hobby, Sport, Book, Food, Game, Pet, Ice cream, and Color. Have each student tape his photograph to the center of his sheet, then fill each section with an illustration of his favorite hobby, sport, book, food, game, pet, ice cream, or color. Display the finished projects on a wall titled "The Classroom Wall Of Fame." Invite students to visit the display to learn about their famous friends!

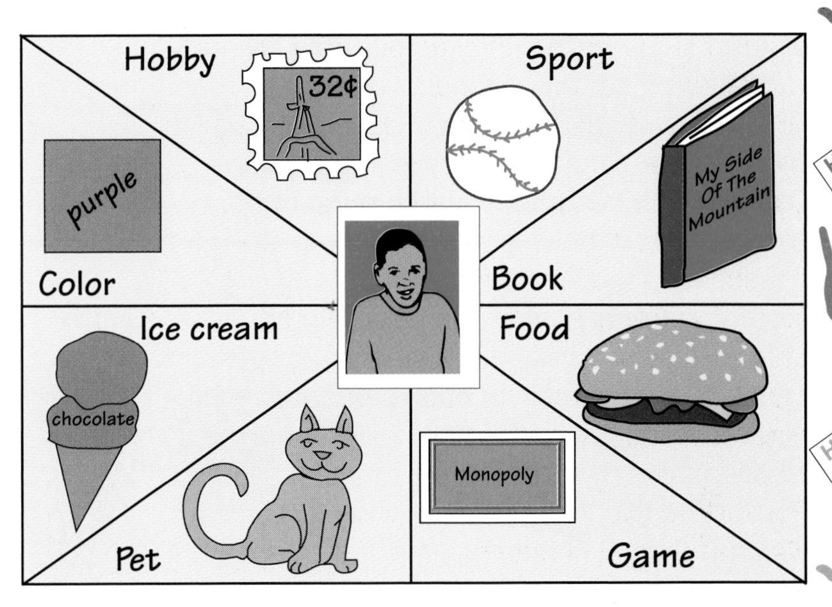

Irene Taylor—Gr. 4
Irene E. Feldkirchner School
Green Brook, NJ

Friendly Faces

Take time to introduce your students to the important, friendly faces who work at their school. Invite the cafeteria manager, janitor, nurse, counselor, and other important employees to visit your classroom during the first week of school. Have each individual introduce himself to the class, explain his job, and tell how he helps make the school a more pleasant place for everyone. Your guests will feel honored, and your students will smile when they see these familiar faces around the school.

Cathy Ogg—Gr. 4
Happy Valley Elementary
Johnson City, TN

HELLO my name is

Autographs, Please!

Your students will feel like movie stars after this getting-acquainted activity! Duplicate and distribute one copy of page 82 to each student. Inform students that the reproducible contains 25 different summer activities or events. Then instruct students to sit in two concentric circles on the floor so that each child in the inner circle is facing a partner in the outer circle. Instruct partners to exchange papers. Then direct each student to find one activity or event listed on the page that she completed during the summer and sign her name in that box. Allow a few minutes for each student to share with her partner some information about the summer experience. Make sure each student gets his original paper back. Then call out, "Rotate," and tell the students in the inner circle to move one space to the left and the students in the outer circle to move one space to the right. Have the new partners exchange papers and repeat the process. Tell students that each box on their papers can be signed by only one student. Continue rotating the circles until the two original partners are facing one another. What a fun way for students to share their summer experiences!

Patricia Twohey—Gr. 4
Old County Road School
Smithfield, RI

Tom

1. Visited Grand Canyon
2. Love football
3. Have 15 brothers and sisters
4. Like reading mysteries
5. Belong to the Boy Scouts

Believe It Or Not!

This icebreaker will have your students acquainted in no time at all! Give each student in your class an index card on which to write five positive or unusual facts about himself. Tell students that four of the five facts should be true and one should be made-up. Have each student introduce himself to the class and read his five facts from his card. After a student has read all five of his facts, have the other students in the class guess which fact is false. Believe it or not, some true facts will be assumed false!

Lori Brandman—Gr. 5
Shallowford Falls Elementary
Marietta, GA

Teacher Passports

Help your students and their parents get to know you better by mailing them a "Teacher Passport." To create your passport, divide an 8 1/2" x 11" sheet of paper into thirds as shown. Program one-third of the passport as a cover. Include a title and an inviting illustration. Next program one-third to include a photograph of yourself and personal information—interests, hobbies, pets. Then program one-third to include school information such as your room number, the school's address and phone number, and any needed student supplies. On the back include a calendar for the first month of school and a class schedule. Duplicate one copy of the passport for each student on brightly colored paper. Fold each passport into thirds, stick it in an envelope, address the envelope, and mail it to the student the week before school starts. Students and parents will appreciate getting to know you before they actually meet you.

Beverly Langland—Gr. 5
Trinity Christian Academy
Jacksonville, FL

What's In The Sack?

Using one of Shel Silverstein's poems will make getting to know your students a breeze! Select four or five small items to share with the class that represent your hobbies and interests. Place the items in a brown lunch bag and display the bag in your classroom. Then read "What's In The Sack?" from *Where The Sidewalk Ends: Poems And Drawings* by Shel Silverstein (HarperCollins Children's Books, 1974). Ask students to guess what each item in your bag represents. For homework give each student a brown, paper lunch bag. Then instruct him to find four small objects at home that represent some aspects of his personality, put them in his bag, and bring the bag back to school the next day. Have the student explain to the class what each object in his bag represents. What a great way to learn about your students!

Julie Eick-Granchelli—Gr. 4
Towne Elementary
Medina, NY

Hot Potato

Here's a "spud-tacular" way for your students to get to know each other. Have your students sit in a large circle on the floor. Decide on a topic, such as brothers and sisters, hobbies, or sports; then start passing a potato or a small ball around the circle. On your signal, whoever is holding the potato must share something about himself related to the given topic. After a few students have shared on the same topic, change the topic and have students continue passing the potato. By the end of the game, your students will know all the hot stuff about their classmates!

Beverly Langland—Gr. 5
Trinity Christian Academy
Jacksonville, FL

I have a sister named Rayna.

It's All In The Bag!

This guessing game is a perfect getting-acquainted activity for the first day of school. Give each student a paper lunch bag and an old magazine. Instruct each student to cut out pictures or words that represent his personality and place them in his bag. Tell students not to write their names on the bags. Collect all the bags and redistribute them to the class, making sure a student does not receive his own bag. Instruct each student to look at all the pictures and words in the bag; then call on one student at a time to show his bag and guess its owner. If a student guesses incorrectly, have other students try to guess the bag's owner. Once all the owners have been revealed, pass each bag back to its original owner. Have each student write his name on his bag, then use markers to decorate the front of the bag. Hang the decorated bags on a bulletin board titled "It's All In The Bag!"

Maureen Winkler—Gr. 5
Winter Springs Elementary
Winter Springs, FL

First-Day Plants

Just like children, plants grow and develop at their own rates. Use this analogy to demonstrate the individuality of each student in your class. On the first day of school, give each student a small potted plant. Supply each student with a variety of art supplies and instruct him to decorate his pot. Tell each student that he is responsible for meeting his plant's needs—water, sunlight, and plant food. Conduct a class discussion on what must be done to care for a plant. At the end of the week, have each student write in his journal about his plant's progress. Culminate this activity after the second week by having each student compare himself to his plant. Give each student a large sheet of newsprint. Then direct each student to draw a picture of himself and a picture of his plant. Instruct the student to write a brief paragraph underneath his illustrations that describes how he is like or different from his plant. Have each student show his illustrations and read his paragraph to his classmates; then post students' artwork around the classroom.

Barbara Samuels—Gr. 5
Riverview School
Denville, NJ

Fitting Your Students To A "T"

Looking for a unique way for students to reveal their personalities? Create a blank T-shirt pattern on a sheet of white paper. Duplicate one copy for each student and distribute the patterns on the first day of school. Provide students with a variety of art supplies, such as markers, crayons, glitter, old magazines, scissors, and glue. Instruct each student to design a T-shirt that represents her personality. Once the T-shirts have been completed, have each student show her shirt and explain what her design represents. Hang a length of clothesline across a bulletin board titled "Fitting Us To A 'T.' " Then staple the T-shirts to the board as if they are drying on the line.

Jill Barger—Gr. 4
Glenwood Elementary
Virginia Beach, VA

Who Am I?

Combine a fun icebreaker with a review of paragraph writing. On chart paper or an overhead transparency, write a paragraph about yourself using the following format: an introduction sentence stating whom you are, three detail sentences giving specific information about yourself, and a conclusion sentence. Read your paragraph to the class; then instruct each student to write his own paragraph, following the same format. Collect the completed paragraphs; then have the entire class stand. Read aloud the three detail sentences from one student's paper without revealing her name. Instruct each student to sit down if the sentences were not read from her paper. Tell the student who is left standing to introduce herself to the class. Then instruct the class to stand again. Give the student who introduced herself another paragraph, and have her read the three detail sentences. Continue the game in the same manner until each paragraph has been read and each child has been introduced.

Maureen Winkler—Gr. 5
Winter Springs Elementary
Winter Springs, FL

Special News Bulletin

Here's a chance for your students to use their reporting skills. Instruct each student to create a list of ten interview questions. Have him use these questions to interview an assigned partner and record his responses. After the interview, have each child write a special news bulletin about his interviewee. Set up an area of your classroom to look like the set of a prime-time news program. Have each student use this set to introduce and give a brief history of the student he interviewed. With this activity everyone becomes the top story!

Cathy Ogg—Gr. 4
Happy Valley Elementary
Johnson City, TN

The Name Game

This name game is the perfect icebreaker for the first day of school! Have your students sit in a large circle on the floor. Start the game by handing a small ball or beanbag to one student. Have that student say her name and then throw the ball to another person. Tell the person who catches the ball that he must repeat the thrower's name and add his own name. Continue until all students have introduced themselves.

Add a little more fun to the game by naming a category such as hobbies. Have the student who catches the ball state his name and a hobby he enjoys that begins with the same letter as his name. Then tell him to throw the ball to another person, and instruct that person to repeat the thrower's name and hobby, then add his own name and hobby (for example, "Bob—baseball, Sally—singing"). End the game and humor your students by trying to correctly repeat each student's name and hobby.

Cathy Ogg—Gr. 4
Happy Valley Elementary
Johnson City, TN

First-Day Tours

Becoming familiar with a new school is often difficult for students. Make this year's tour an excursion! Pass out several compasses before giving your students a tour of the school. Each time the line changes direction, have one of your students call out the cardinal direction in which you are headed—north, south, east, or west. When you return to the classroom, review your tour by using the cardinal directions. For example: "Is the library north or south of our classroom?" Then group students into pairs, and give each pair a large piece of construction paper and markers. Instruct each pair to draw a map of the school showing the location of each place visited on the tour. Then have each pair present its map to the rest of the class. These activities will provide a great review of compass points and a fun first-day tour!

Barbara Samuels—Gr. 5
Riverview School
Denville, NJ

Classroom Management

Shoe-Bag Mailboxes

Organization will be a shoo-in with this easy tip! Hang a plastic, over-the-door shoe divider on the wall or on a closet door in your classroom. Assign students mailboxes by labeling each pocket with the name of a different student. Have a student helper place any papers that need to go home in each student's mailbox. Also direct each student to place assignments to be taken home in his mailbox each day. Remind each student to collect his mail as he exits your class for the day. What a great way to keep important papers from being lost in the shuffle!

Lori Sammartino—Gr. 4
Clayton Traditional Academy
Pittsburgh, PA

Record Keeping Made Easy

Keep important information right at your fingertips with this practical suggestion. Purchase an inexpensive notebook; then record each student's name on a different page. Record personal data—phone numbers, addresses, emergency contacts—on each student's page. Document student behavior in the notebook and record communication with parents. Use a paper clip to attach important notes to a student's page. This notebook will quickly become one of your most valuable resources!

Lara Marshall
1462 Stratford Lane
Winston Salem, NC 26842
(910)555-7691

Richie Mihans
243 Country Club Road
Winston Salem, NC 26846
(910)555-4568

David Reitz—Gr. 4
Glenwood Elementary
Virginia Beach, VA

Tea Is For Teacher

Take a little time while preparing your back-to-school student supply list to think about your own needs. Dedicate a corner of your supply cabinet for teacher essentials. Purchase flavored tea bags or hot chocolate, aspirin, candy, tissues, cough drops, and other essentials to make your days run smoothly. Store these items in a basket in your supply cabinet. Having these added comforts on hand makes working late hours a lot easier!

Julie Eick-Granchelli—Gr. 4
Towne Elementary
Medina, NY

Folder Frenzy

Looking for a way to organize student work folders so that they are orderly and easily accessible? Purchase a hanging file folder for each student and two filing crates. Assign each student in your class a different number and record it on his file folder. Label one filing crate "1–15" and the other "16–30." Labels will vary according to the number of students in your class. Direct students to file their folders numerically in the appropriate crate. Place each crate in a different area of the room to avoid traffic problems. Post a list of student names and numbers near each crate until students have learned their numbers.

Irene Taylor—Gr. 4, Irene E. Feldkirchner School, Green Brook, NJ

Daily Assignment Log

Enlist the help of student volunteers to keep their absent peers up-to-date on classroom activities. Decorate a notebook and title it "Daily Log." Appoint a different student to be the keeper of the log each day. Instruct the log keeper to record in the log a summary of each activity completed in class, each assignment given, and any other instructions. Have the log keeper sign the log and return it to you at the end of the day; then reward her with a small treat of some sort for her efforts. Give the daily assignment log to each student returning from an absence so she can see what she missed. Also use the log as a reference during parent conferences.

Karen Arnett
Chesapeake, VA

Silent Signals

Avoid unnecessary interruptions and distractions in your classroom with this successful management technique. Create several silent signals for students to use when they need to ask for permission to complete a task. Keep the signals simple and limited in number so students can remember them easily. For example, have each student hold up her pencil if she needs to sharpen it. Direct each student to signal when she needs to use the bathroom by holding up two fingers. Respond to the student with a nod or your own silent gesture of approval if the time is appropriate. You'll be amazed at how much this easy-to-use system cuts down on interruptions!

Rosemary Spaw—Gr. 4
Glenwood Elementary
Virginia Beach, VA

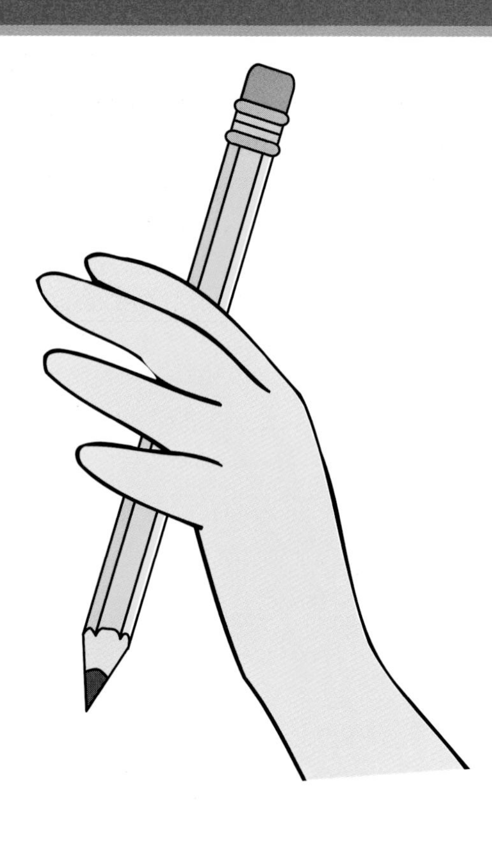

Reusable Displays

Ever wish you could save a favorite bulletin board just as it is for use during the next school year? With this practical idea, you can! Cut burlap, denim, or another inexpensive fabric to fit the size of your bulletin board. Pick coordinating fabrics for letters, designs, and borders to put on the bulletin board. Iron permanent bonding material to the back of each piece of material. Then cut out letters, designs, and borders from the bonded cloth with fabric scissors or pinking shears. Finish the display by ironing the letters, designs, and borders to the background material. Use the bulletin board when you need it; then fold or roll it up and store it in a plastic bag for the next year. What a super way to save time and money!

Marilyn Davison—Grs. 4–5
River Oaks School
Monroe, LA

Clothespin Participation

Try this easy system to make sure all students get an opportunity to respond in your class. Purchase a package of clothespins and label each clothespin with the name of a different student in your class. Clip the clothespins around the edge of a round plastic butter or sherbet tub. Each time you need a response during class time, pull a clip off the tub and call on the student whose name it features. Then toss the clothespin in the tub to avoid calling on the student more than once. Continue calling on students in this fashion until every child has had an opportunity to respond. Reverse the procedure, pulling clothespins from the tub and pinning them on the rim, to allow each student an additional chance to respond. You'll have no more complaints from students who say you never call on them!

Nancy Murphy—Gr. 5
Converse School
Beloit, WI

Another Day, Another Group

Do you ever have trouble remembering the names of the different cooperative groups in your class? Avoid this problem by naming each cooperative group after a day of the week. This system also helps out in other areas of classroom management. On Mondays, have the Monday group be line leaders, special helpers, and the first to leave at the end of the day. Repeat the process for the Tuesday, Wednesday, Thursday, and Friday groups on their respective days. Each group has its own special day of the week, and you'll never forget a group's name or who goes next.

Wanda McLaurin—Gr. 5, Bangert Elementary, New Bern, NC

Wednesday Group

While You Were Out

Make updating students who are returning from an absence much easier with this simple filing system. Purchase a hanging file crate or box and five hanging file folders. Label each of the file folders with a day of the week—Monday through Friday. File leftover handouts in the appropriate folders. When a student returns to school, instruct him to check the folders and collect any missed assignments. What an easy way to stay on top of things!

Patricia Altman—Gr. 6, Lewis M. Klein Middle School, Harrison, NY

Hassle-Free Snacktime

Keep snacktime from turning into a chaotic affair with this practical suggestion. Decorate a box and label it “Snacks.” Remind each student to clearly label his snack at home before bringing it to school. Direct each student to place his snack for the day in the box as he enters the classroom. Then appoint a student helper to pass out the snacks at the appropriate time. No more feeding frenzy at snacktime!

Wanda McLaurin—Gr. 5, Bangert Elementary, New Bern, NC

See-Through Organizer

Make distributing, collecting, and storing supplies for group activities a breeze with the help of several plastic organizers. Purchase a see-through, plastic organizer with a lid for each cooperative group in your class. Place commonly used materials in each box such as markers, scissors, a ruler, a glue stick, and crayons. Add special materials needed for a particular lesson to each box ahead of time. Assign a student from each group to be in charge of retrieving and returning the supply box for his group. Since the boxes are see-through, you'll be able to check at a glance that all materials are accounted for!

Patricia Altman—Gr. 6

Managing Student Journals

Journals are an excellent way to improve student writing skills, but keeping up with 25–30 journals is another story! Color-coding can make managing the task a lot easier. Assign a different color to each day of the week, Monday through Friday. Then evenly divide students' journals into five piles, making one pile for each day of the week. Code the journals in each day's pile with a corresponding colored sticker or marker. Each day collect journals by that day's assigned color. Now you only have five or six journals to check and respond to each day.

Irene Taylor—Gr. 4, Irene E. Feldkirchner School
Green Brook, NJ

First-Day Photos

The first day of school is a great opportunity to capture your students at their best, so why not capture it on a roll of film? Take two photographs of each student or have double prints made of your film. Use one photograph to make a back-to-school display featuring the entire class or attach the photo to a piece of the student's work to display for open house. Place the second photo on a birthday card to give to each student on her birthday.

Wanda McLaurin—Gr. 5
Bangert Elementary
New Bern, NC

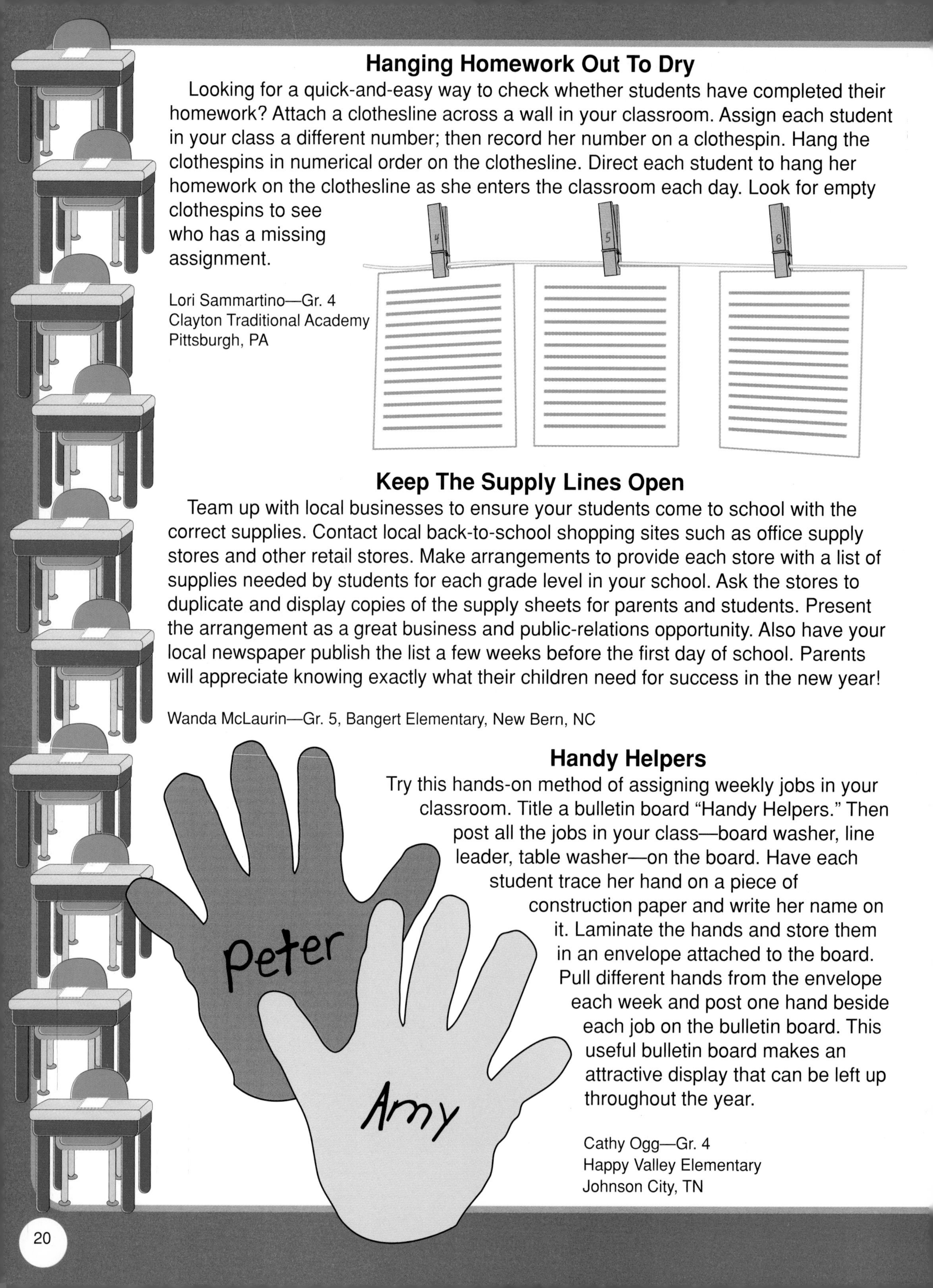

Hanging Homework Out To Dry

Looking for a quick-and-easy way to check whether students have completed their homework? Attach a clothesline across a wall in your classroom. Assign each student in your class a different number; then record her number on a clothespin. Hang the clothespins in numerical order on the clothesline. Direct each student to hang her homework on the clothesline as she enters the classroom each day. Look for empty clothespins to see who has a missing assignment.

Lori Sammartino—Gr. 4
Clayton Traditional Academy
Pittsburgh, PA

Keep The Supply Lines Open

Team up with local businesses to ensure your students come to school with the correct supplies. Contact local back-to-school shopping sites such as office supply stores and other retail stores. Make arrangements to provide each store with a list of supplies needed by students for each grade level in your school. Ask the stores to duplicate and display copies of the supply sheets for parents and students. Present the arrangement as a great business and public-relations opportunity. Also have your local newspaper publish the list a few weeks before the first day of school. Parents will appreciate knowing exactly what their children need for success in the new year!

Wanda McLaurin—Gr. 5, Bangert Elementary, New Bern, NC

Handy Helpers

Try this hands-on method of assigning weekly jobs in your classroom. Title a bulletin board "Handy Helpers." Then post all the jobs in your class—board washer, line leader, table washer—on the board. Have each student trace her hand on a piece of construction paper and write her name on it. Laminate the hands and store them in an envelope attached to the board. Pull different hands from the envelope each week and post one hand beside each job on the bulletin board. This useful bulletin board makes an attractive display that can be left up throughout the year.

Cathy Ogg—Gr. 4
Happy Valley Elementary
Johnson City, TN

Special-Delivery Folders

Keeping each parent informed of his child's progress is a snap with the help of special-delivery folders! Send home papers in a folder labeled "Special Delivery" every two weeks. Include an itemized list of the assignments that should be in the folder, along with the accompanying work. While you distribute students' folders and work samples, have each student write a letter to his parents detailing what he has learned in the past two weeks. Direct each student to place the letter in his folder and take it home for review by his parents. Require that each student return his folder with a parent signature. This is a great way for students to reflect on their progress while keeping parents informed!

Lori Sammartino—Gr. 4
Clayton Traditional Academy
Pittsburgh, PA

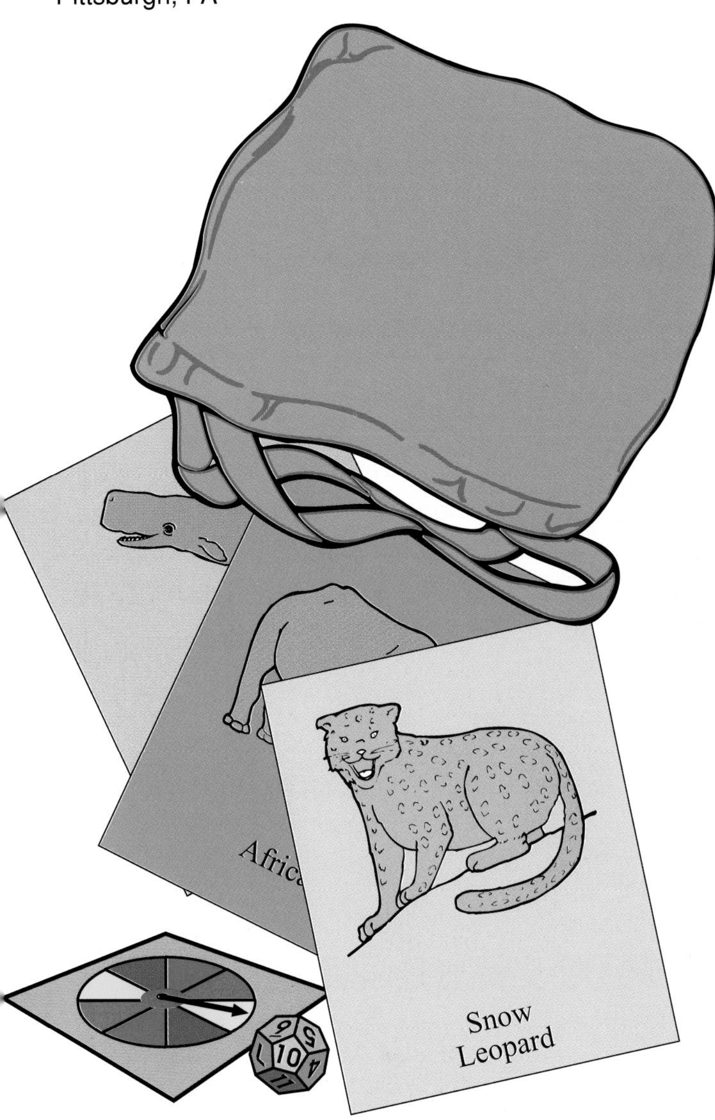

Tote-Bag Learning Centers

Turn ordinary tote bags into mobile learning centers for your classroom with this creative tip! Store learning-center activities and games in separate tote bags. Be sure to include clear instructions and all necessary materials in each bag so a student can independently complete the enclosed activity. Hang the tote bags from coat hooks and allow students to complete the bagged activities during their free time. Direct each student to return materials to the tote bag when he is finished with a task. Send a bag home with a student occasionally so he can complete an activity with his parent. You'll never have to worry about locating missing pieces again!

Cathy Ogg—Gr. 4
Happy Valley Elementary
Johnson City, TN

Bulletin Boards

Welcome your students to a cool school year with this fun bulletin board. Enlarge the shark pattern on page 83 and mount it on the board. Enlarge and duplicate the sunglasses pattern on page 83 for each student. Have the student cut out the pattern, assemble it, and write his name on the two earpieces as shown. Tape a piece of green Reynolds® Plastic Wrap to the back of each pair of glasses to serve as lenses. Then mount the sunglasses on the board.

Cathy Ogg—Gr. 4, Happy Valley Elementary, Johnson City, TN

Tip your hat to a great class with this student-created bulletin board. Duplicate one copy of the baseball-hat pattern on page 84 for each student. Have him draw a self-portrait in the left section of his hat, illustrate a special interest in the right section, and write his name on the bill. Post the completed hats on a bulletin board for students to enjoy.

Cathy Ogg

Grab a slice of your students' lives with this mouthwatering bulletin board. Duplicate a class set of the watermelon pattern on page 84. Have each student write about a summer experience on her pattern. Instruct her to lightly color the pattern green and pink, then cut it out. End the activity by serving a snack of crisp watermelon.

Terry Healy—Gifted K–6, Eugene Field Elementary, Manhattan, KS

Students will yield when they see their names on this bulletin board! Enlarge a class set of traffic-sign patterns on page 85 and label each sign with a different student's name. Mount assorted school supplies—such as rulers, pencils, and scissors—around the students' names to add the finishing touches!

Julie Eick-Granchelli—Gr. 4, Towne Elementary, Medina, NY

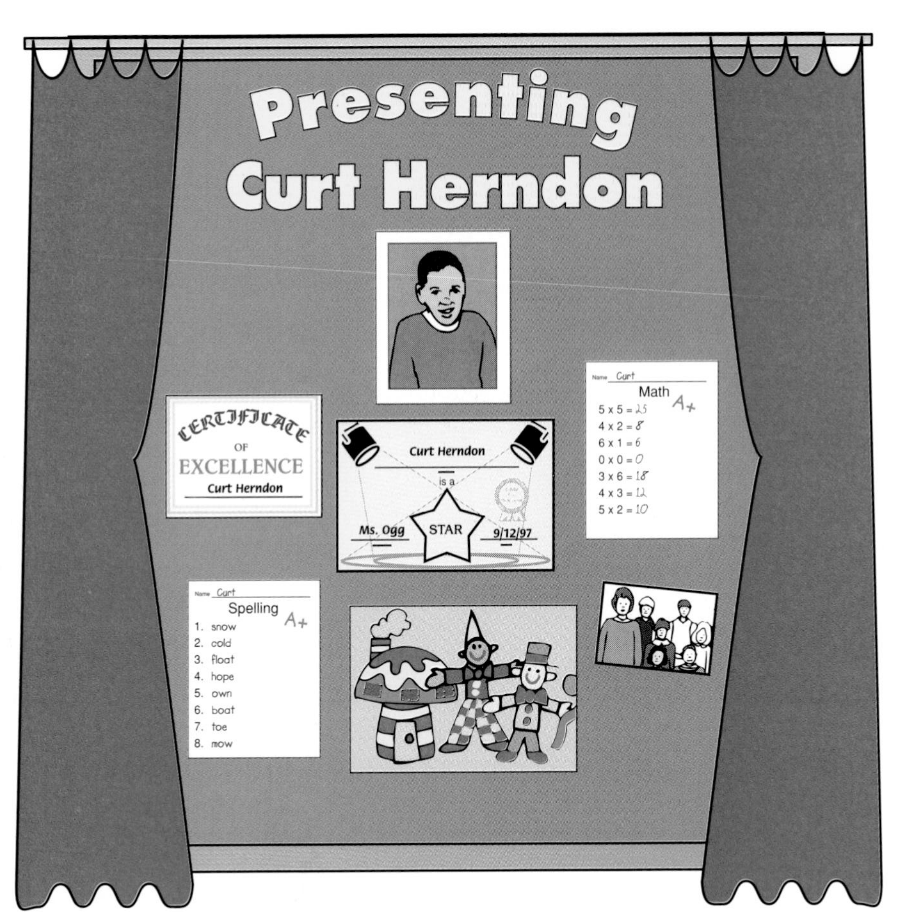

Each student will have a chance to be the main attraction of this bulletin board! Create a stagelike display by hanging inexpensive curtains on both sides of a bulletin board. Duplicate a class supply of the star award on page 85. Each week fill out an award for a different student and post it on the board. Instruct the student to bring in special items and family photographs to display on the board.

Cathy Ogg—Gr. 4
Happy Valley Elementary
Johnson City, TN

Help your class choose the right tools to be successful students. Mount a large construction-paper toolbox in the center of a bulletin board. Enlarge and duplicate the tool patterns on page 86. Write one strategy for success in your classroom on each tool; then post each tool on the bulletin board.

Patricia Altman—Gr. 6, Lewis M. Klein Middle School, Harrison, NY

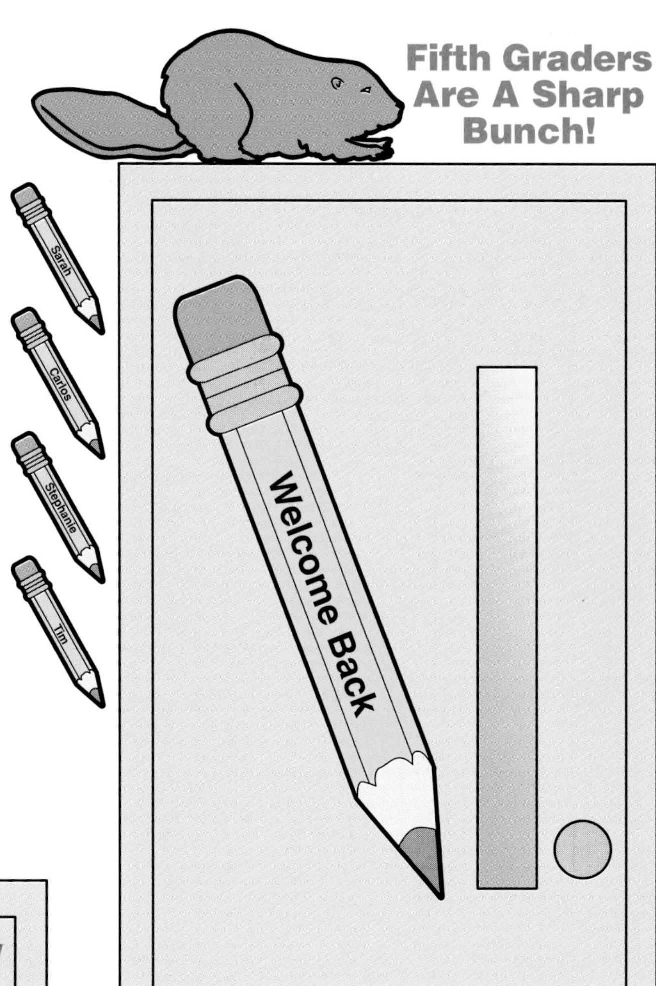

This "a-door-able" decoration is sure to welcome your new class! Post a large construction-paper pencil on your classroom door. Then hang a construction-paper beaver above your classroom door as shown. Duplicate a class supply of the pencil pattern on page 86. Write each student's name on a separate pattern; then post the pencil patterns around the door frame. Everyone walking by your classroom will definitely get the point!

Colleen Dabney—Gr. 6
Williamsburg Christian Academy
Williamsburg, VA

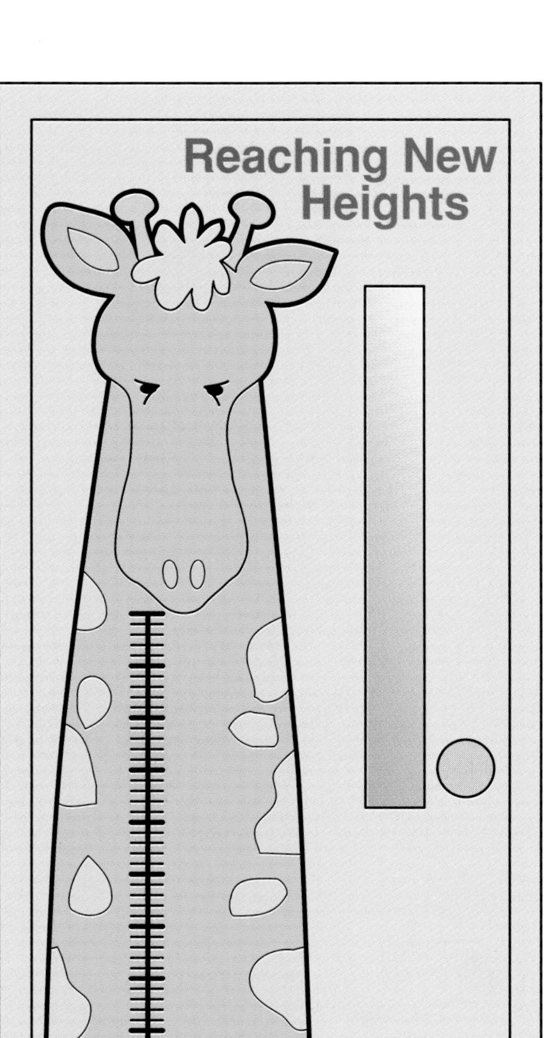

Get out your yardstick for this door display! Post an enlarged copy of the giraffe pattern (page 87) on the back side of your classroom door. Use a yardstick to label measurements on the giraffe in two-inch increments. Measure each student's height; then post a photo of each child next to his current height. Students will enjoy keeping track of how much they grow throughout the year!

Colleen Dabney

Piece together a cooperative group of students with this student-made display. Cover a bulletin board with paper; then use a marker to divide the board into puzzle pieces—one for each student. On each piece, mount a student's photograph and label it with her name. Have students write under their pictures about how they can work together as a class.

Beverly Langland—Gr. 5, Trinity Christian Academy, Jacksonville, FL

Don't kick off the school year without having your students set their game plans! Create two football goalposts from construction paper and mount them at opposite ends of a green-covered bulletin board. Duplicate a class supply of the football pattern on page 87. Have each student write one goal for the year and the steps needed to achieve that goal on his pattern. Post the patterns on the board as shown.

Terry Healy—Gifted K–6, Eugene Field Elementary, Manhattan, KS

Launch a new year with this explosive bulletin board. Enlarge the rocket-ship pattern on page 88 and attach it to the board. Duplicate a class supply of the star patterns (page 88) on yellow construction paper. Label each star with a different student's name. Post the stars around the rocket ship for an out-of-this-world display!

Patricia Altman—Gr. 6, Lewis M. Klein Middle School, Harrison, NY

Set aside a small bulletin board for the daily lunch count. Divide the board into one section for each lunch choice. Add magazine pictures of appropriate foods to each labeled section. Have each student use a marker to label a 3" x 5" index card with his name. Laminate each card for durability. Every morning have each student use a pushpin to post his lunch-choice card in the appropriate section of the board.

Irene Taylor—Gr. 4
Irene E. Feldkirchner School
Green Brook, NJ

Spring into a class discussion on similarities and differences among class members with this unique bulletin board. Create several posters with headings such as "Bookworms," "Sports Fanatics," and "Pizza Eaters." Mount the posters on a bulletin board and invite students to write their names on each poster that applies to them.

Barbara Samuels—Gr. 5, Riverview School, Denville, NJ

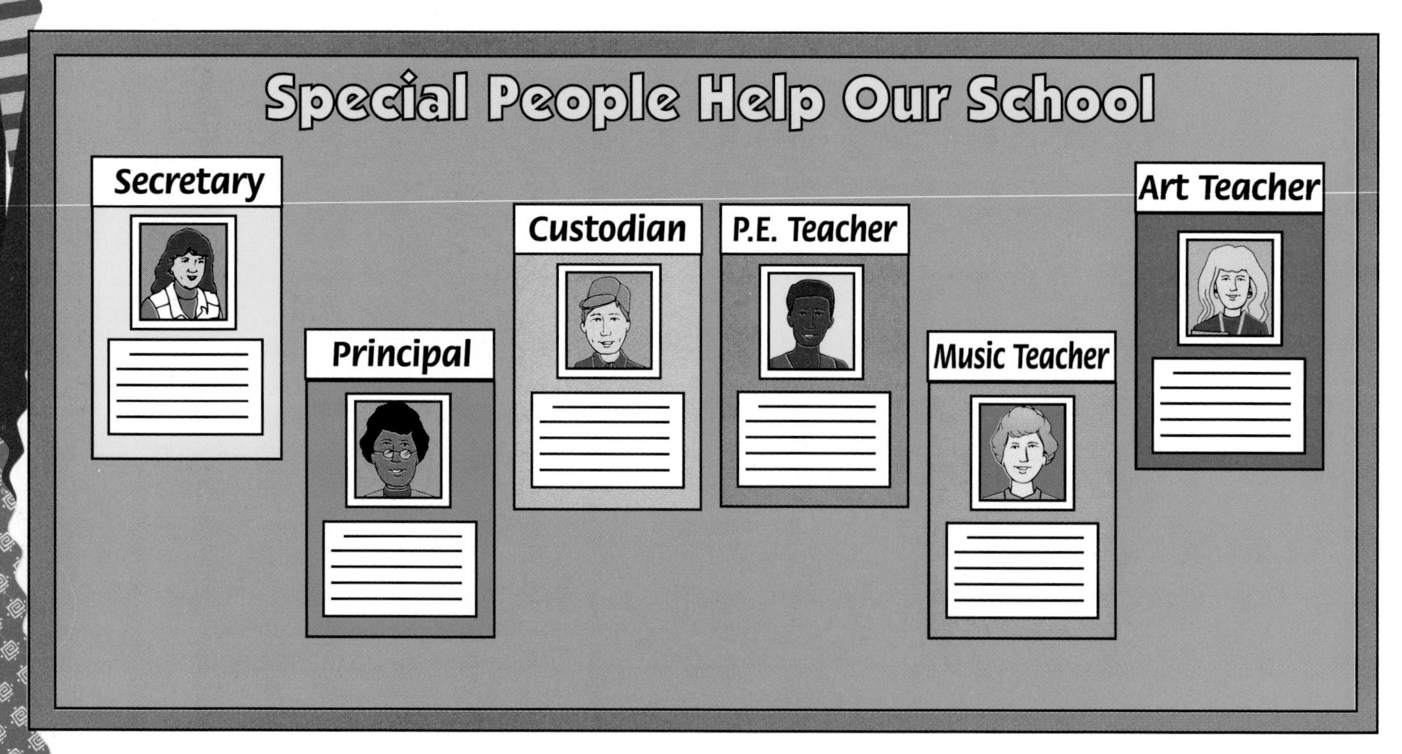

Introduce your students to school employees with this informative bulletin board. Mount pictures of the principal, the secretary, the custodian, and other employees on separate sheets of construction paper; then post each mounted photo on a bulletin board. Add a job title and description to each photo to give students a greater awareness and appreciation for the special people who work at their school.

Patricia Twohey—Gr. 4, Old County Road School, Smithfield, RI

Give students a hand with this colorful display. Cover a bulletin board with bright paper. Post one blank sheet of notebook paper on the board for each student. Have each student use water-based paint to make handprints on the board above one sheet of notebook paper; then have the student write her name above her handprints. Replace the blank sheets of notebook paper with work from each student.

Julie Eick-Granchelli—Gr. 4, Towne Elementary, Medina, NY

Create this door display on the first day of school. As each student arrives, have her trace and cut out her footprints on a piece of construction paper, then label the footprints with her name. Post each set of footprints on the classroom door and encourage students to take a big step into a new year!

Beverly Langland—Gr. 5, Trinity Christian Academy, Jacksonville, FL

Open House Activities

Reflective Invitations

Jazz up your open-house invitations this year. Supply each student with a piece of 9" x 12" construction paper, a 4" x 4" square of aluminum foil, glue, and markers. Direct each student to fold his paper in half like a card. Tell the student to glue the square of aluminum foil to the front of the card and draw a decorative frame around it. Then have the student write "We want you…" below the frame. On the inside of the card, have the student finish the sentence with "to attend open house." Instruct the student to also include important details such as date, time, and place. These unique cards will reflect your desire and your students' desire to have parents attend this important beginning-of-the-year event.

Julie Eick-Granchelli—Gr. 4
Towne Elementary, Medina, NY

Parent Pop Quiz

Surprise parents with a pop quiz at open house. Supply each student with one 9" x 12" sheet of construction paper, old magazines and newspapers, glue, and scissors. Then have each student scour the magazines and newspapers for pictures and words that describe her personality. Direct the student to cut out the pictures and words, and then create a collage by gluing them to her sheet of construction paper. Instruct the student not to put her name on the collage. On the day of open house, have each student tape her collage to the top of her desk before leaving for the day. As each parent enters the classroom, tell him that he must find his child's seat by identifying which collage represents his child's personality. Post a seating chart in the front of the room so each parent can quickly check if he has located the correct desk. Parents will enjoy this little pop quiz on their children's personalities.

Maureen Winkler—Gr. 5, Winter Springs Elementary
Winter Springs, FL

SUPER! Awesome! SUPER! Awesome!

Dear Susan,

I enjoyed meeting your teacher, and I am very proud of all your hard work!

Love,
Mom

Special Messages

Try this noteworthy tip at this year's open house. Place decorative notepaper and colorful pens and stickers at a table. At the end of the evening, encourage each parent to use the materials to write a special message to his child. Then have the parent leave the note on his child's desk. Write a note for each child whose parent could not attend and place it on his desk. The next morning, watch as each of your students delights in the special message received from a caring adult.

Julie Eick-Granchelli—Gr. 4
Towne Elementary
Medina, NY

Valuable Volunteers

Open house is the perfect time to get parents involved in their children's learning. Create a "Valuable Volunteers Invitation." Include a list of ways that each parent can volunteer in the classroom such as helping with special projects, tutoring students, assisting on field trips, and donating goodies for classroom parties. Distribute the invitations to parents as you welcome them at the door. Have parents fill out the forms before they leave. Voila! You have a ready list of valuable volunteers!

Colleen Dabney—Gr. 6
Williamsburg Christian Academy
Williamsburg, VA

Valuable Volunteers Invitation

- Cut out laminated artwork
- Tutor students in the classroom
- Help monitor centers
- Help on field trips
- Read aloud a novel to students
- Share an expertise associated with a job or hobby

Covering All The Bases

It's on the tip of your tongue—you have one more item on your list of things to tell parents the night of open house, but you just can't remember it. Does this scenario sound familiar? Prevent this from happening by sending home an open-house questionnaire. Include topics on the questionnaire such as homework and grading policies, discipline procedures, parent/teacher contact, and a class schedule. Also include an area for other specific parent questions and suggestions. Send a copy of the questionnaire to each parent a week or so prior to open house. Ask each parent to complete the questionnaire and return it to you as soon as possible. Compile the information into one list, and you'll be sure to cover all your bases at open house!

Terry Healy—Gifted K–6
Eugene Field Elementary
Manhattan, KS

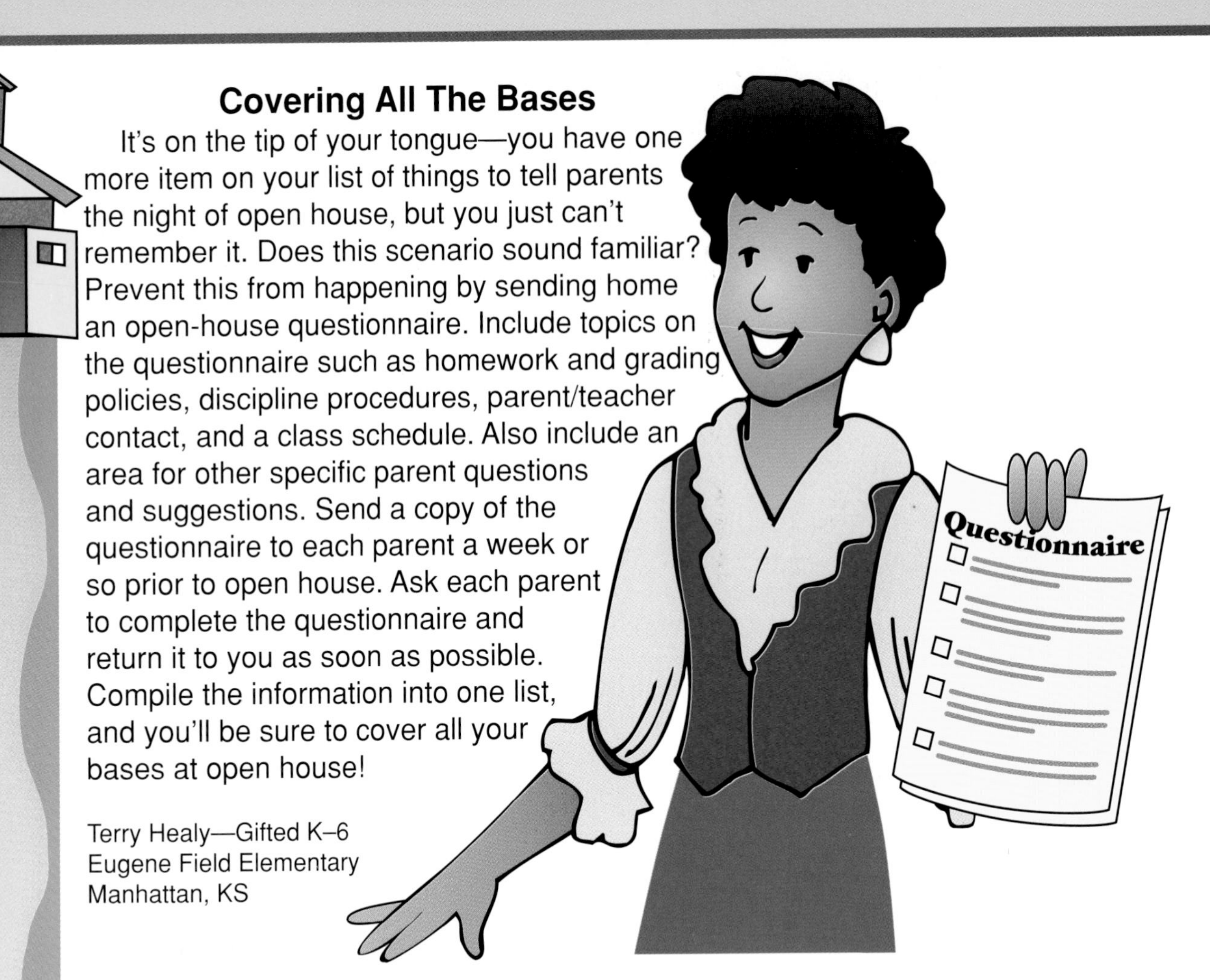

A Picture-Perfect Idea

This first-day activity can help make your open house picture-perfect! In one corner of your classroom, hang a photo backdrop made from bulletin-board paper or a large piece of decorative cloth. Place items in front of the backdrop that students will use during the year such as a microscope, globe, bookcase, or computer. Take a picture of each student standing in front of the backdrop, as well as a class photo. Post the individual pictures on each student's desk or on a bulletin board. Also post the class photo in a welcoming hallway display for open house. After open house, save the photos for student recognitions, special class projects, and parent gifts.

Julie Eick-Granchelli—Gr. 4, Towne Elementary
Medina, NY

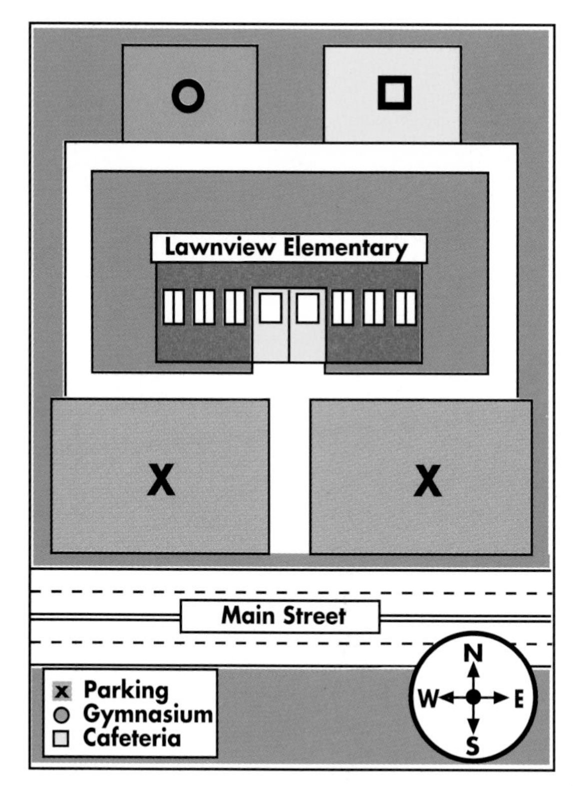

Mapping The Way

Here's an innovative way to incorporate map skills into your open house. Take your class on a tour of the school; then give each student a large piece of white construction paper and have him create a map of the school. Instruct the student to include a layout of the school's grounds and buildings, a legend, and a compass rose on the map. After the maps are made, have each child bring his map home and tell his parent that she must use the map to locate the classroom at open house—even if the parent already knows the room's location. If the parent finds the room successfully, reward the child the following day with a special treat. This is a great incentive for students to create accurate maps and to get parents involved in their children's learning.

Maureen Winkler—Gr. 5, Winter Springs Elementary
Winter Springs, FL

Take Note!

Open house is often a blur of activity. As a result, there is never enough time to inform parents about all of the wonderful things going on in your classroom. Here's a simple way to solve this problem, and get your students involved in the process.

On the day of open house, give each student a piece of decorative notepaper. Direct the student to think of five to ten things about her classroom that she wishes her parent to know. Have her write a brief message to her parent on the piece of notepaper. Encourage the student to write the message in an inviting manner such as "Don't forget to check out our Native American dioramas in the library!" or "Take a look at the terrific personal narrative in my writing portfolio!" Have each student tape her message on the top of her desk. Each parent will appreciate the personal note and will be amazed at how busy her child has been during the first few weeks of school!

Julie Eick-Granchelli—Gr. 4, Towne Elementary
Medina, NY

- *Don't forget to check out our Native American dioramas in the library!*
- *Take a look at the terrific personal narrative in my writing portfolio!*
- *Look at how many stickers I have posted on our class "Great Work" chart. Isn't it great?*
- *Go to the art room so you can see my detailed sketches.*
- *Be sure to look at the science experiment we are conducting. We're observing how different environmental conditions affect a plant's growth. It's really interesting!*

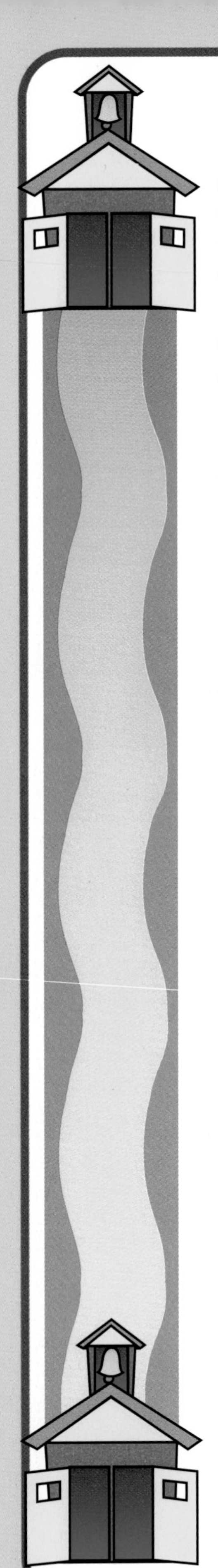

High-Flying Nametags

Open house is held the night before school begins in many places. As a result, most students are eager to attend the open house with their parents in order to see what the classroom looks like, find out who is in their class, and locate where they are going to sit. Create a festive display and show each student where she will sit using helium balloons.

Purchase a helium balloon for each student. Write the student's name on a balloon using a permanent black marker and tie it to the back of her seat. When the student arrives, she will be able to easily spot her seat. Invite the student to take her balloon home at the end of the evening. The remaining balloons will quickly let you know which students were unable to attend open house.

Phyliss Grady Adcock—Gr. 5, West Lake Elementary
Apex, NC

Calling All Parents!

Who among us doesn't need a little incentive to come out to a school function after a long, hard day's work? To help entice more parents to attend your open house, plan an evening of fun-filled activities such as those listed below. Then call parents and invite them personally or send a handwritten invitation. Be sure to tell them about the exciting events you have planned for the evening.

- Greet parents at the door and offer some light refreshments.
- Hold a classroom raffle. As each parent arrives, have him fill out a ticket. Draw a name at the end of your presentation and give out a simple prize.
- Have a grade-level competition for the highest parental attendance. Announce the winning class before the end of the evening and reward parents and students with a special treat.
- Have your students perform a skit or give a short presentation.
- Involve parents in a humorous role play about school.
- Give each parent a homework pass. Tell the parent to use it on a night when he and his child wish to have the "evening off."
- Solicit coupons from local businesses. Put together a "Treat Yourself" coupon booklet just for parents.

Jill Barger—Gr. 4, Glenwood Elementary, Virginia Beach, VA

Video Stress-Buster

How do you ease the stress of "opening-night jitters" before open house? Try creating a student-centered informational video! Begin by determining what information you want to cover at open house such as the daily schedule, homework and grading procedures, and your discipline policy. Prepare an informational skit in which each student plays a part. Encourage students to dress for their parts and choose props suitable for the skit. Rehearse the skit several times, and then "roll the tape."

On the night of open house, invite parents to sit back and watch the show as your students serve popcorn and drinks. Parents will gain valuable classroom information while they watch their children perform. You'll be able to "catch your breath" while your students inform and entertain their parents.

David Reitz—Gr. 4, Glenwood Elementary
Virginia Beach, VA

Instant Replay

Here's a great way for parents who were unable to attend open house to actually see what they missed. On the night of open house, set up a camcorder in your classroom. Ask a school volunteer to videotape your presentation as well as parents asking questions about your classroom policies and procedures. Send a note home to parents who were unable to attend open house informing them of the video and encouraging them to check out the video to watch at their convenience. Parents will appreciate not only the valuable information given in the video, but also your efforts to include them in their children's back-to-school night.

Barbara Samuels—Gr. 5
Riverview School
Denville, NJ

Parent Communication

Ringing In The New School Year

You're just a phone call away. So take advantage of this opportunity to personally phone each student on your class list a few days before school begins. Introduce yourself to the person answering the phone at each home and explain the intent of your call. Ask to speak to the parent or guardian first if a child answers the phone. Make the conversation brief and tell each student you look forward to seeing him on the first day of school. This is also an excellent time to inform the parent and child of any needed classroom supplies, and to recruit parent volunteers for the classroom. What a great way to start the year off with parents and students on your side!

Sandra Lowery—Gr. 4
MacArthur Elementary
Ft. Leavenworth, KS

Makin' A Molehill Out Of A Mountain

Everyone is familiar with the avalanche of paperwork that must be sent home on the first day of school! Keep your students organized by sending home the mountain of papers in a large, manila envelope. Have each student decorate her envelope and write her name in permanent marker on the front. Then have the student fill her folder with any papers that need to go home. Direct the student to deliver the envelope to her parents, have her parents review the contents, and return any necessary forms to you in the same folder. Reuse the envelopes for other important deliveries throughout the year.

Wanda McLaurin—Gr. 5
Bangert Elementary
New Bern, NC

Pick A Peck Of Pocket Folders

Did you know that student folders are great resources for teaching important math skills as well as being a vital element of your parent communication system? Keep parents informed of their children's progress each week with a simple pocket folder. Design a weekly cover sheet as shown in the illustration. Duplicate a supply of the cover sheet and attach one to each student's folder. Use the folders to introduce the concept of *averaging* to your students. At the end of each week, have each student list the numerical grade for each assignment in the folder under the appropriate subject heading on his cover sheet. Instruct the student to total each column, then divide each total by the number of grades in each column. At the end of the grading period, have students use each weekly average to find an average for the entire grading period. This process also helps give parents an idea of how well their children are doing academically in school.

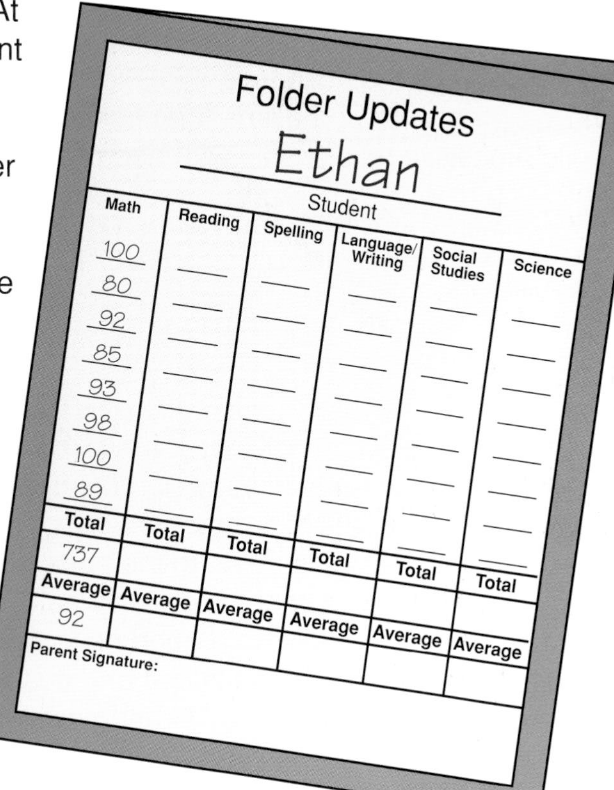

Folder Updates

Ethan

Student

Math	Reading	Spelling	Language/ Writing	Social Studies	Science
100					
80					
92					
85					
93					
98					
100					
89					
Total	Total	Total	Total	Total	Total
737					
Average	Average	Average	Average	Average	Average
92					

Parent Signature:

Martha Woods—Gr. 5
Riceville Elementary
Riceville, TN

Drop Them A Line

Looking for a new way to keep parents informed of their children's positive accomplishments? Purchase some colorful stationery that your students would find humorous. Think of something positive about each child at least once during the year and mail him a note. In your note encourage the student to continue with the positive behavior. Also tell the student to hang on to the note and any future positive-behavior notes he may receive for a special raffle at the end of the year. During the last week of school, place a large fishbowl on your desk. Tell students to bring in any positive-behavior notes they have received since the beginning of the year and place them in the fishbowl. Purchase three or four special prizes for the raffle. On the last day of school, draw three or four cards out of the bowl. If a student's name is drawn more than once, put it back and select another name. Students and parents will love getting this motivational mail and the excitement of the end-of-the-year raffle!

Maureen Winkler—Gr. 5
Winter Springs Elementary
Winter Springs, FL

A Parent's Point Of View

Open the lines of communication early in the school year with this informative parent survey. After all, who knows their children better than parents? Duplicate page 89 for each student in your class. Instruct the student to have his parent fill out the form and return it to school within the first week of school. This survey will give you information on the academic and social needs of each child from the parent's point of view. Parents will appreciate the chance to give you their input. What a great way to build a positive relationship with each child's parent and receive valuable feedback!

Patricia Twohey—Gr. 4
Old County Road School
Smithfield, RI

Extra! Extra! Read All About It!

Want a creative way to keep parents up-to-date on the latest school and class news? Have students generate their own class newsletter. Spend the first few weeks of school introducing students to the parts of a newspaper. Invite a reporter or editor from your local newspaper to explain what is involved in creating a daily newspaper. Then teach the "Five Ws" of a good newspaper article—who, what, when, where, and why. Finally discuss the layout and design of a newspaper. Have your class come up with regular sections for the newsletter such as upcoming events, great achievements, birthdays, class needs, and school news. Assign a different group of students each month to publish the newsletter. Within each group, assign students the roles of reporters, editors, typesetters (word processors), and layout designers. Have one student in the group act as the newsletter manager, helping anyone who needs it, setting up interviews, and resolving problems.

Maureen Winkler—Gr. 5
Winter Springs Elementary
Winter Springs, FL

The Glenwood Gazette
Volume 1 September 1997
School News
UPCOMING EVENTS
Class Needs
GREAT ACHIEVEMENTS
School News
Birthdays

Phone Home!

Ensure that your initial phone contact with parents runs smoothly with a little advance planning. Duplicate a supply of the “Phone Call Data Sheet” on page 90. Before each call, record the purpose of the call and any important information or comments you would like to share with the parent. Also write down important information the parent shares with you during the course of the conversation. Save the phone call data sheet for future reference. Use additional copies of the sheet to plan out follow-up phone calls throughout the year. You'll be surprised at how a few well-planned phone calls can relieve first-day jitters and make your year run a whole lot smoother!

David Reitz—Gr. 4
Glenwood Elementary
Virginia Beach, VA

Electronic Connections

Use the latest advances in technology to open the lines of communication between yourself and parents. At open house ask parents who have access to electronic mail to provide you with their E-mail addresses. Instead of writing notes or making phone calls, send E-mail. You won't have to worry about playing phone tag, and you can be sure your messages will get to their final destination in a timely fashion.

Patricia Altman—Gr. 6
Lewis M. Klein Middle School
Harrison, NY

Nothing's Better Than A Letter!

How can you quickly keep in touch with parents on a weekly basis? Enlist the help of each student by having her write a weekly update letter. Begin the writing exercise by reviewing the format of a friendly letter; then have students brainstorm activities and events from the week. Record these events on the board. Then have each student write a letter to her parents detailing the week's events. Parents will look forward to getting this informative weekly letter and keeping up with what their child is doing.

Maureen Winkler—Gr. 5
Winter Springs Elementary
Winter Springs, FL

Monthly Calendar Mania

Why should you have to do all the work? Use a desktop publishing program such as ClarisWorks 4.0® or The Print Shop® to create informative monthly calendars. Monthly calendars are an excellent way to keep parents and students informed of upcoming events in your classroom. Include test dates, units of study, due dates, and other important events. Decorate each calendar with appropriate seasonal clip art. Provide each student with two copies of the calendar—one to post at home and one to keep at school. Hand out the upcoming month's calendar on the last Monday of the current month. Have students mark unexpected events and assignments on their calendars as they occur.

Maxine Pincott—Gr. 4
Oliver Ellsworth School
Windsor, CT

October 1997

Sunday	Monday	Tuesday	Wednesday	Thursday	Friday	Saturday
			1 CMT Math part #2	2	3 Assembly	4
5 Reading Nutrition Solar System	6	7	8 Book order due Math test	9	10 Spelling test	11
12 Reading Nutrition Whale Watch	13 Field trip	14	15 Math test	16	17	18
19 Northeast Nutrition Reading	20	21	22	23 Book project due	24	25
26 Reading Nutrition Solar System	27 Field Trip	28	29 Social Studies test	30	31	

Week In, Week Out

Many students find it difficult keeping up with their pencils, much less keeping up with due dates and long-range projects. To meet the needs of those students in your class who find long-range planning difficult, use a desktop publishing program to make a generic weekly calendar. List the days of the week on the left-hand side; then outline your schedule for the week by keying in specific activities planned for each subject. Also use the calendar to list vocabulary words or bonus words for the week. Provide each student with a weekly calendar each Monday. Parents and students will appreciate the clearly outlined objectives and due dates.

Maxine Pincott—Gr. 4
Oliver Ellsworth School
Windsor, CT

Week Of November 9, 1997

Sunday 9	Bonus Words: accept, except, affect, effect, a lot	
Monday 10	Spelling Grammar Reading Mimi: Whale Watch Journal	
Tuesday 11	Spelling: Sentences 1–10 Grammar: Pronouns and Adjectives Social Studies: Read Geography Journal: Reflect on the Day Reading: Read Chapter 12	
Wednesday 12	Grade 5 Interactive Project Health: Sources of Nutrients Process Writing Journal: Reflect on the Day	
Thursday 13	Spelling: Sentences 11–20 Grammar: Subjects and Predicates Reading: Read Chapter 13 Fathoms Journal: Reflect on the Day	
Friday 14	Spelling Test Maps and Navigation Science: Solar System Journal: Reflect on the Week	
Saturday 15	10/21 Mystic Seaport Keep on target with your Solar System Project!	

Dear Parent,

Dear Parent,

Weekly Progress Reports

Keeping parents informed of their child's progress is one of a teacher's biggest challenges! To make the process a little easier, label a file folder for each student in your class. Each week duplicate the "Weekly Report" form from page 90 for each student. Fill in the information, and attach the report to her folder. On Monday have each student put her graded papers from the previous week in her folder. Then record the number of papers that are contained in the folder on the appropriate blank of the "Weekly Report." Complete the rest of the form to update the parent of his child's progress. Have students get their parents to sign the form and return the emptied folder to school the following day.

Cathy Ogg—Gr. 4
Happy Valley Elementary
Johnson City, TN

Positive Discipline

Cotton Balls

Looking for a new way to monitor class behavior? How about using cotton balls! Obtain a clear, plastic container and purchase a bag of 300 cotton balls. Each time your class exhibits good behavior—such as walking quietly in line, displaying lunchroom manners, or being cooperative at specials—have a student add ten cotton balls to the container. When the class has earned all 300 cotton balls, celebrate with a popcorn party. As the year progresses, make it more challenging to earn the cotton balls. Watching the cotton balls pile up will motivate your students to work towards positive group behavior!

Meg Turner—Gr. 5
Seawell Elementary
Chapel Hill, NC

Check It Off

Reinforcing positive student behavior on a regular basis can be difficult. Use a monthly checklist to keep track of praise given to each student. Create four columns on a sheet of paper; then label the columns accordingly: Name, Phone, Note, and Reward. List your students' names in the first column and use the other three columns on the chart to record a check each time you call a parent, send a note home, or give a student a sticker or other reward for great behavior. Make one copy of the chart to use for each month of the school year. Use the chart to make sure each child has been recognized for his positive behavior at least once. With this method no student will ever be overlooked!

Jill Barger—Gr. 4
Glenwood Elementary
Virginia Beach, VA

Name	Phone	Note	Reward
Lara		✔	
Charles	✔		✔
Frankie	✔		
Georgia			✔
Kim		✔	
Rodney	✔	✔	
Kenny			✔
Lucy		✔	✔

Think-About-It Cards

Have you ever removed a student from a group due to poor behavior and then forgotten to discuss with that child why she was removed? Solve this problem by creating "Think-About-It" cards. Title a half-sheet of paper "Think About It." Then write the following questions: "What was I doing?", "Why is this behavior inappropriate?", and "How can I improve my behavior?" Leave space underneath each question for the student to respond in writing. At the bottom of the page, create a blank for the student's signature, the teacher's signature, the parent's signature, and the date. Duplicate a supply to keep handy at your desk. The student answers each question during her time-out, signs the card, and discusses the situation with the teacher. If the circumstances are serious, send the card home for the parent to sign and return. Giving the student time to think and respond in writing helps her calm down and take responsibility for her actions.

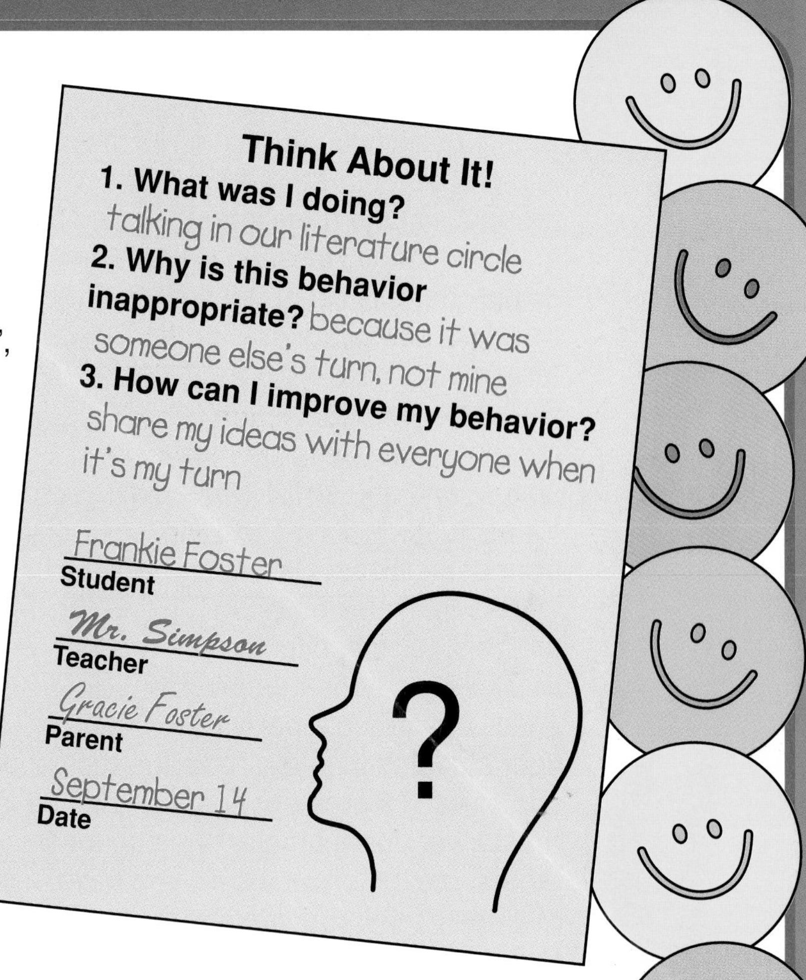
Think About It!
1. What was I doing?
talking in our literature circle
2. Why is this behavior inappropriate? because it was someone else's turn, not mine
3. How can I improve my behavior?
share my ideas with everyone when it's my turn

Frankie Foster
Student
Mr. Simpson
Teacher
Gracie Foster
Parent
September 14
Date

Points For Popcorn

Searching for a way to instill positive behavior in your students? Use the "Points-For-Popcorn" method. Label 27 poker chips with the following point values: 5 points *(20 chips),* 10 points *(5 chips),* and 25 points *(2 chips).* Place all the chips in a bag or container. Designate two or three times each day to evaluate class behavior. If the class displays appropriate behavior, allow one student to reach into the bag and pull out a chip. Write the point value from the selected chip on the chalkboard or other visible location; then put the chip back into the bag. Each time a new chip is pulled from the bag, add the point value from the chip to the existing total on the chalkboard. When the class reaches its goal of 200 points, treat your students to a popcorn party. Students will anxiously watch the point total climb towards 200 while you enjoy a well-behaved class!

Rosemary Spaw—Gr. 4
Glenwood Elementary
Virginia Beach, VA

It's 25 points!

25

Recipe For A Happy Classroom

Here's a tasty way to introduce classroom rules on the first day of school! Briefly explain to your students the need for classroom rules; then divide the class into groups of three or four. Instruct each group to list the rules it feels should be enforced in the classroom. Have each group share its list of rules; then have the class compile a master list. Now for the tasty part!

Place a large bowl, a measuring cup, a large mixing spoon, and one small paper cup for each student on a table in front of the class. Use ingredients such as stick pretzels, raisins, bite-sized crackers, and other small, dry snacks to create a party mix. Tell your students that you have the recipe for a happy classroom. Measure out one cup of each ingredient and add it to the large bowl as you read each rule from the master list (for example, one cup for lining up quietly, one cup for respecting others, etc.). Continue until you have included all the rules from your master list. Mix up all the ingredients in the bowl and serve it to your students in paper cups. Voilà—a happy classroom!

Patricia Twohey—Gr. 4, Old County Road School, Smithfield, RI

Star Box

Reach for stars with this positive discipline strategy! Create a grid on an 8 1/2" x 11" sheet of white paper by dividing it into one-inch by one-inch boxes. Then draw a simple star pattern in each box. Duplicate several copies of this grid and have a volunteer cut out the stars for you. Each time you see a student displaying positive behavior, give him a star. Have the student write his name on the star and drop it into a brightly wrapped box. On Friday draw a few stars from the box and reward those students with special treats. Students quickly learn that the more stars they receive, the better their chances of winning!

Malinda Borum—Gr. 4, Glenwood Elementary
Virginia Beach, VA

Your Ticket To A Well-Behaved Classroom

Looking for a quick-and-easy way to encourage positive student behavior? Use good-behavior tickets as motivation. Purchase inexpensive tickets from a craft store. Then paste one library-card pocket for each group or table of students in your class on a sheet of poster board. Place a ticket in each group's pocket for exhibiting behaviors such as turning in all homework, having quick transitions between subjects, and staying on task. At the end of the week, reward the group that has received the most tickets with a treat. Students will work hard at improving their behavior and will anxiously await each Friday's announcement of the winning group!

Tickets For Good Behavior!

Group 1 Group 2 Group 3

Group 4 Group 5 Group 6

Maxine Pincott—Gr. 4
Oliver Ellsworth School
Windsor, CT

Question Box

Help students solve their own problems with this cool idea. Cover a shoebox or other small container with colorful wrapping paper; then cut a small opening in the top of the box. Place the box in a central location. Put a stack of blank paper strips by the box. Instruct each student who has a problem or question to write his concern on a paper strip and put it in the question box. Once a week check the box and conduct a classroom discussion about the questions and concerns in the box. Then help students find possible solutions for each question. Using this strategy lets children know that you are interested in their concerns, and that they have the ability to solve many of their own problems. After a few weeks, you will find less bickering and more students working peacefully in your classroom!

How do you deal with a bully?

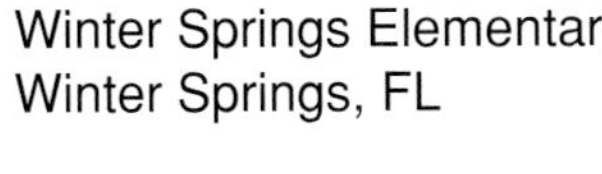

Maureen Winkler—Gr. 5
Winter Springs Elementary
Winter Springs, FL

STUDENT MOTIVATION

SUPER STUDENT

YOU'RE A MATH WHIZ!

YOU'RE GREAT!

Shining Students

Give your students a chance to shine by being "Star-Studded Students Of The Week." Duplicate a class supply of the "Star-Studded Student" form on page 91. Then assign each student a different week during the school year to be the star. Send a "Star-Studded Student" form home with the selected student on the Friday before her scheduled week. Instruct the student to fill out the form with her parents, detailing information on items she plans to bring, special guests she plans to invite, and personal information she plans to share with the class. Encourage the student to bring in items such as family photographs, special collectables, favorite books, souvenirs, and awards or trophies. Arrange an area of the room where the student can display her special items. Set aside a time for the student to show the items to the class. Have her classmates draw pictures or write poems, songs, or letters for the student. Collect the writings and artwork, add a decorative cover, and bind them together with yarn or ribbon. Present the book to the student on Friday, topping off the weeklong salute to the star.

Patricia Twohey—Gr. 4, Old Country Road School, Smithfield, RI

Plant A Birthday Smile

Students whose birthdays fall before the school year begins will appreciate this blooming good idea! Obtain a small plant pot for each of these students. Write each student's name on a pot along with a happy-birthday message using a colorful paint pen. Then place a square of Styrofoam® in each pot. Stick several lollipops in each Styrofoam® square; then fill each pot with Easter grass or shredded green paper. Place a pot on the desk of each student whose birthday fell before school began. This sweet treat is sure to bring a smile to those students who often feel their birthdays aren't recognized. Inform the other students that they too will receive special treats when their birthdays arrive.

Beverly Langland—Gr. 5, Trinity Christian Academy, Jacksonville, FL

Responsibility Counts

Students are eager to help their teachers. Why not take advantage of this and assign each student to be your assistant for one week? Discuss with your students that a teacher's job includes many responsibilities such as planning and preparing lessons, keeping up with the day's schedule, grading papers, and communicating with colleagues and parents. Explain that being a teacher also has many rewards and privileges; then ask students to give examples of what they view as rewards of the job.

Tell each student that for one week he will become a teacher's assistant. The assistant will be responsible for helping you perform various teacher-related tasks, and will receive rewards for his services. Duplicate a class supply of the "Responsibility Counts!" form on page 91. Each Friday complete one form for the student you've selected to be your assistant the following week. Have a brief conference with the student to discuss the responsibilities and privileges listed on the form. You'll appreciate the extra help, and the student will enjoy the extra responsibilities and privileges.

Elizabeth Tanzi—Gr. 5, Burr Intermediate School, Commack, NY

A Banner Year!

Name: Hannah

B — I will earn at least a B average in each subject area this year.

I will keep my room clean and do the dishes two times a week.

I will make one new friend.

A Banner Year!

You'll be off to a successful year with this banner idea! Discuss with your students that in order to achieve a dream, goals must be set. Encourage each student to set three goals for the year such as "I will earn at least a B average in each subject area" or "I will make the girl's basketball team." Then duplicate and distribute the banner on page 92 to each student. Have the student write her three goals on the banner. Next have the student decorate her banner with symbols associated with her goals. Extend a piece of string or rope from the ceiling; then hang each student's banner on the string for all to read.

Colleen Dabney—Gr. 6
Williamsburg Christian Academy
Williamsburg, VA

SUPER STUDENT

YOU'RE A MATH WHIZ!

YOU'RE GREAT!

Teamwork Is No Puzzle

How many times have you seen one student in a group doing all the work? Help your students visualize the importance of each team member with this activity. Obtain six or seven sheets of 9" x 12" construction paper (each sheet a different color); then cut each sheet into four puzzle pieces. Divide your students into teams of four. Give each team four puzzle pieces of the same color, an 18" x 24" sheet of white construction paper, a black marker, glue, and colorful markers or crayons.

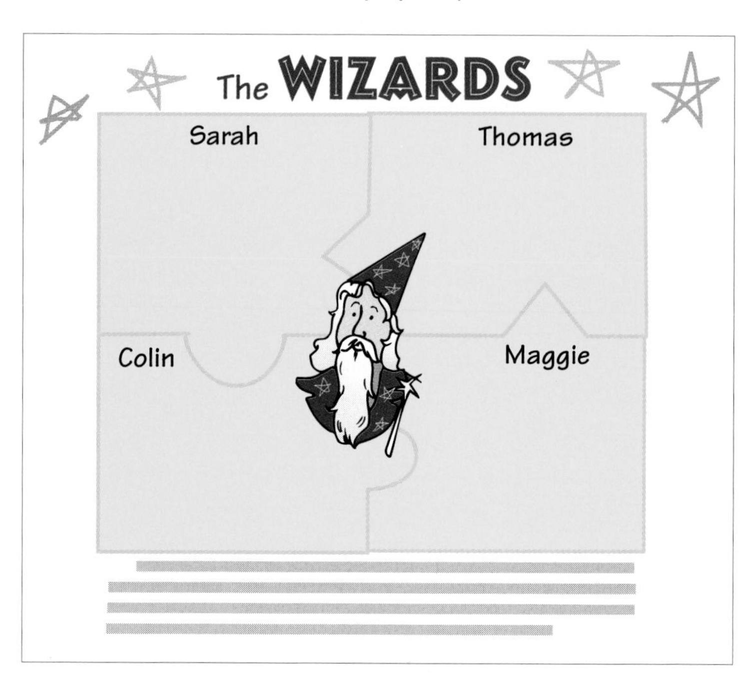

Direct each team member to take one puzzle piece and print her name with a black marker across the top. Next instruct the team to connect the pieces, then glue the completed puzzle to the center of its white sheet of paper. Challenge each team to create a team name and design a team logo. Have the team draw the logo on its puzzle and write its team name above the puzzle on the white paper. Finally instruct the team to write a brief paragraph below the puzzle, explaining how the team is like a puzzle. Have each team read its explanation to the rest of the class; then display the puzzles on a wall or bulletin board.

Patricia Twohey—Gr. 4, Old Country Road School, Smithfield, RI

CLASSROOM TUTORS

Reading	Math	Science
Dan	Tasha Greg	Chris
Social Studies	**Spelling**	**Language**
Davin Rachel	Sarah Simon	Brianna

Get By With A Little Help From A Friend

What student doesn't love taking on the role of teacher? Help build student character and promote high self-esteem by encouraging your students to become classroom tutors. Make a list of classroom subjects. Encourage each student to sign his name under a subject in which he feels comfortable tutoring other students. Post the list in a designated spot in the classroom. Anytime a student needs a little extra help in a particular subject, he can consult the list to find a friend who is an "expert" in that area. The tutor, student, and teacher will feel good about getting a little help from a classroom friend.

Elizabeth Tanzi—Gr. 5, Burr Intermediate School, Commack, NY

Put An End To Put-Downs

Sensitize your students to the widespread problem of put-downs with the following activity. Ask each student to write an often-heard put-down on a slip of paper. Collect the slips and write the responses on the board. Discuss with students why they think people use put-downs, what emotional reaction put-downs cause, and where they often hear people using put-downs. Point out to students that popular TV shows—especially sitcoms—often use put-downs. Identify which sitcoms are programmed for that evening. Then send a note home to each parent informing him of the class discussion on put-downs, and requesting the parent to help his child select one age-appropriate sitcom to view that evening. Instruct the parent to help his child record the number of put-downs heard during the program. Also include a section on the note for the parent to check and return if he does not want his child to participate in the activity. The next day, organize the data into a class graph, identifying which sitcoms contained the most and least number of put-downs. Challenge each student to come up with a positive phrase for a put-down used in the sitcoms.

Elizabeth Tanzi—Gr. 5, Burr Intermediate School, Commack, NY

Word Power

Positive words have a way of promoting rewarding relationships. Remind students of this every day—visually! Generate a list of positive words and expressions with the class. Give each student a 12" x 18" sheet of white construction paper. Have the student choose one of the words or expressions to write on his paper in large block letters. Finally have the student color and cut out the word or phrase. Laminate each student's positive message; then display them around the room for all to see and use. Continue to add more positive words and phrases to the display by periodically repeating this activity throughout the year.

Elizabeth Tanzi—Gr. 5

Rewarding Good Homework Habits

Here's a sharp idea that will point your students in the right direction for good homework habits! Create a pencil pattern and make a copy for each student. Also give each student a 4" x 6" index card. Instruct the student to use a ruler to divide the card into six equal squares. Then have the student cut out the squares and hole-punch the top of each square. Next direct the student to write each letter of the word *reward* on a separate card. Have each student write her name on her pencil pattern, decorate it, and cut it out. Post each student's pencil pattern on a bulletin board titled "Sharp Students Earn Rewards." Attach each student's six cards, blank-side-up, to the bulletin board with a pushpin below the student's pencil. Each time a student completes a week's worth of assignments, have her turn over a card and pin it letter-side-up under her pencil pattern. When the word *reward* is revealed, present the child with a special treat.

Cathy Ogg—Gr. 4, Happy Valley Elementary, Johnson City, TN

Designer Homework

Here's an assignment that will be met with a rousing cheer from your class—student-designed homework! After introducing the day's lessons, divide the class into small groups. Assign each group a subject for which to design a homework assignment. Explain to each group that its assignment must meet the following criteria:

- the assignment must relate to the lesson taught that day
- the assignment must take no more than 15 minutes to complete
- the assignment should be motivating
- an answer key should be included, if needed

The following day, collect and evaluate each group's assignment; then have each group explain its assignment to the class. This designer homework will empower and motivate each student, as well as reflect an understanding of the lesson.

Phyliss Grady Adcock—Gr. 5, West Lake Elementary, Apex, NC

Homework Lotto

Here's just the ticket to encourage better completion of homework assignments. After collecting a daily homework assignment, randomly choose one or two papers from the pile. Reward each student whose paper was pulled with a treat such as a piece of candy, a special privilege, or a homework pass. Your students will be more motivated to complete all of their assignments when they know there's a chance of being the lucky winner!

Irene Taylor—Gr. 4, Irene E. Feldkirchner School, Green Brook, NJ

Homework Stamp Of Approval

This idea is sure to earn a stamp of approval from your students! For each student, set a weekly goal for a specific number of completed homework assignments. Tell each student that if he reaches his goal, he will earn a reward. Next give each student a large index card. Direct the student to write his name and homework goal at the top of his card and keep it at his desk. Each day, stamp the student's card with a decorative rubber stamp for each completed homework assignment. On Friday, invite each student who met his goal to write his name on a slip of paper. Collect each slip in a paper bag. Choose one or two names from the bag and reward each student whose name was drawn with a prize. Keep the remaining names in the bag from week to week. Each time a student reaches his goal, have him put his name in the bag. The student soon realizes that his chances of winning increase each time he reaches his homework goal and puts his name in the bag.

Irene Taylor

Student Organization

Label It!

Do all the papers you return ever make it home to Mom and Dad? Use self-sticking labels to help students organize their weekly work before it is taken home. Type various positive messages on the labels such as "My favorite assignment!", "My best paper!", "Look at this!", and "I'm proud of this one!" If they're available, use a computer and label printer to quickly reproduce a page of labels for each student. Have each student use the labels to flag specific papers for his mom and dad. Students will take more pride in showing off their work, and fewer papers will get crammed into bookbags!

Cathy Ogg—Gr. 4
Happy Valley Elementary
Johnson City, TN

On The Road To Success

Use this goal-setting activity to get your students on the road to successful organization! First discuss with your class how to set realistic goals and how to decide what steps are needed to achieve those goals. Have each student set a goal for the first grading period and write four steps needed to reach that goal. Next give each student one copy of the patterns on page 93. Instruct him to cut out each wheel and write his goal in the wheel labeled "I'm Rolling Toward...." Then instruct the student to write one step for reaching his goal in each section of the divided wheel. Tell the student to number each step. Have the student use crayons or colored pencils to decorate both wheels. Then direct each student to place the wheel containing his goal on top of the wheel containing the steps and secure the two wheels with a brad as shown. Mount the wheels on a bulletin board titled "The Road To Success—Drive Carefully!" Turn each wheel so that it shows the first step. After a student completes the first step, have him turn the wheel to reveal the next step he must take to reach his goal. Continue in the same manner until each goal is reached.

I'm Rolling Toward...
Author Of The Month
(Goal)
Step 1
Review the writing process and brainstorm a list of writing ideas.

Elizabeth Tanzi—Gr. 5
Burr Intermediate School
Commack, NY

Homework IOUs

Put the responsibility for tracking missing assignments in your students' hands! Each month duplicate one copy of the IOU form on page 94 for each student. Store the forms alphabetically by students' last names, in a 5" x 8" file box in an accessible area of the classroom. When a student comes to class without an assignment, send him to the IOU file box and have him complete the first three columns on his form. When the student turns in the late assignment, record the date on his IOU. At the end of the month, send the IOUs home for parents to sign and return. Place the signed forms in your classroom files as a record of parent communication and each student's homework habits.

Lori Sammartino—Gr. 4
Clayton Traditional Academy
Pittsburgh, PA

Waste Not, Want Not

Do your students come to school on the first day with school supplies for the entire year, only to run out after the first month? To help students become less careless and more conscientious of how they use their supplies, give each student a gallon-size, Ziploc® freezer bag. Have each student place an extra package of notebook paper, extra pencils and pens, and other extra supplies in his bag. Label each student's bag with his name using a black permanent marker. Collect the bags, and store them in a cabinet or closet. When a student runs out of a specific item, pull out his bag and let him get the needed item. Parents will love this waste-decreasing and money-saving idea.

Marilyn Davison—Grs. 4–5
River Oaks School
Monroe, LA

Did You Notice?

Demonstrate the importance of good observation skills with this fun activity! On the first day of school, bring with you an entirely different change of clothes, including shoes and accessories. While the students are at lunch, change into the new set of clothing without telling your class. When the class returns from lunch, ask them if they notice anything different. Then challenge students to write a paragraph describing what you were wearing before lunch. Encourage students to try and describe the former outfit from head to toe. Have each student read his paragraph to the rest of the class. Then pull out the former outfit and show students exactly what you were wearing. The perplexed looks on your students' faces will provide the perfect opportunity to introduce the importance of being very observant when conducting science experiments!

Phyliss Grady Adcock—Gr. 5
West Lake Elementary
Apex, NC

When Is Lunch?

"When is lunch?" "Do we have art today?" "What time is music?" Do your students bombard you with questions like these each day? Help your students practice sequential ordering as they learn the classroom schedule. At the end of the first day of school, write a list of the day's activities on the chalkboard in random order. Instruct students to put the list of activities in the order that they were completed. At the end of the week, repeat the same activity, but this time use a list of activities from the entire week. Soon students will know exactly what to expect from each day's schedule!

Phyliss Grady Adcock—Gr. 5
West Lake Elementary
Apex, NC

lunch
math
outside
PE
science
social studies
D.E.A.R.
writing
reading
snack
recess

Calendars Galore

Looking for a way to help your students keep up-to-date and organized? Mount a large monthly calendar on the wall of your classroom; then duplicate a small monthly calendar for each student to place in her notebook. Write all test dates, upcoming projects, special events, and other important dates on the wall calendar, and have your students transfer the information to their personal calendars. Teach your students how to use the calendar to plan ahead for projects and tests by referring to the calendar frequently and updating it weekly. Instruct students to take their calendars home to be signed by their parents each weekend. This strategy will improve students' organizational skills and keep their parents informed of classroom activities!

Patricia Altman—Gr. 6
Lewis M. Klein Middle School
Harrison, NY

Study Buddies

Two heads are better than one! Take advantage of this phenomenon and help your students stay organized throughout the year by grouping students into study-buddy pairs. Every afternoon, instruct each study buddy to check his partner's assignment pad for accuracy and his backpack to make sure his partner is taking home the proper materials to complete the assigned work. This keeps all students on target and makes for a less hectic classroom at the end of each day.

Barbara Samuels—Gr. 5
Riverview School
Denville, NJ

Let's Get Organized

Need a strategy to help parents, teachers, and students work together to teach organizational skills? Add an assignment book to each student's school supply list. Each day have students record the date, the day's assignments and activities, and any homework assignments in their assignment books. Have each student leave space for parent comments, and then instruct him to have his parent sign the book each night. Periodically check each student's assignment book and award stickers to the students who have been keeping up with the daily entries. If a student receives four stickers in a row, reward him with a special treat or homework pass. These assignment books are also great for parent-teacher communication.

Maureen Winkler—Gr. 5
Winter Springs Elementary
Winter Springs, FL

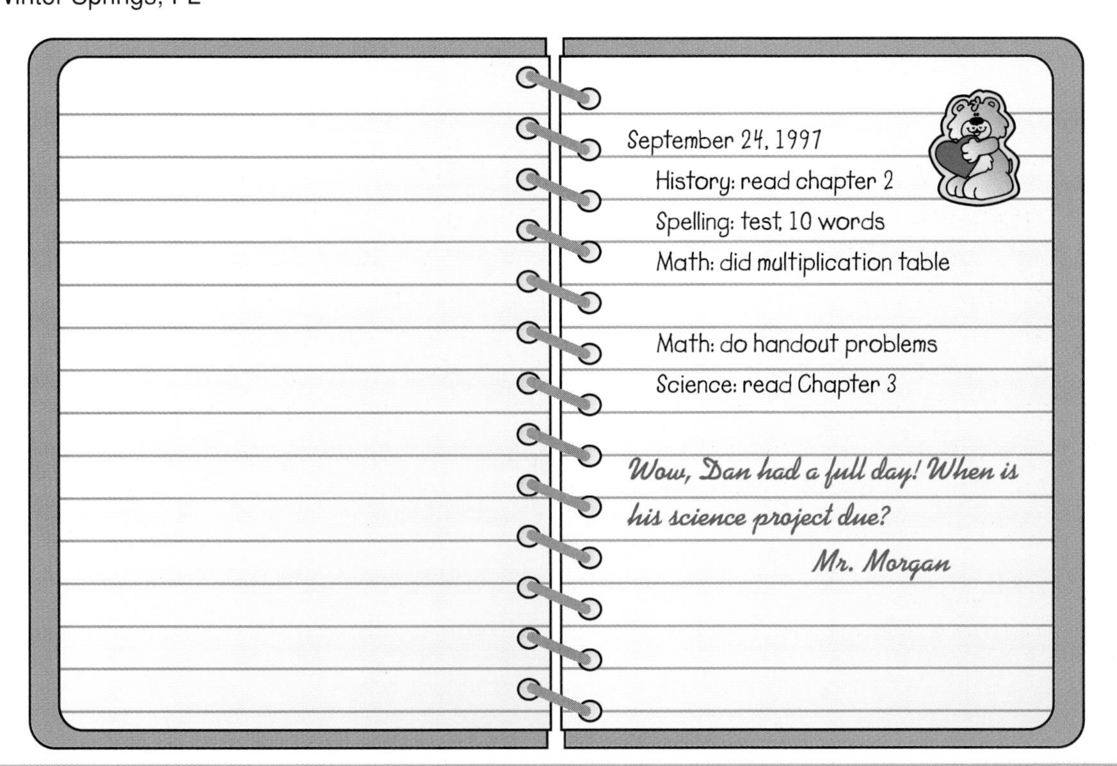

Novel Nametags

Here's a great way to dress up student nametags and encourage students to share a little something about themselves. Use a pencil to print each student's name in block letters (approximately 3" x 5") on a 6" x 24" strip of tagboard; then give each student his nametag. Challenge the student to transform each letter of his name into a picture of something that represents his personality. For example, a student with the letter *A* in his name who likes to go camping can turn the letter *A* into a tent. Have the student extend the picture by adding elements of his choice, such as a campfire, trees, and animals. After the student has sketched a picture for each letter in his name, have him outline the letters with a fine-tipped black marker. Then have the student color each of his pictures with crayons or colored pencils. Have each student introduce himself and explain each picture on his nametag; then display each student's nametag on the front of his desk.

Terry Healy—Gifted K–6, Eugene Field Elementary, Manhattan, KS

Cards That Show You Care

Create a lasting treasure for grandparents on their special day. Inform your students that National Grandparents Day falls annually on the first Sunday in September following Labor Day. Give each student a 9" x 12" sheet of construction paper, scissors, glue, a supply of fabric, ribbons, glitter, and beads. Direct each student to fold the paper in half and design a greeting card to send to her grandparent or an elderly friend or family member. Encourage the student to think of an imaginative message that expresses her love and appreciation. Have the student begin her message on the outside of the card and continue it on the inside of the card. For example, have the student write, "Grandpa…You're the apple of my eye!" or "My heart belongs to…Grandma!" Next instruct the student to illustrate and decorate her card using the various craft supplies. Grandparents and students will benefit from these caring expressions.

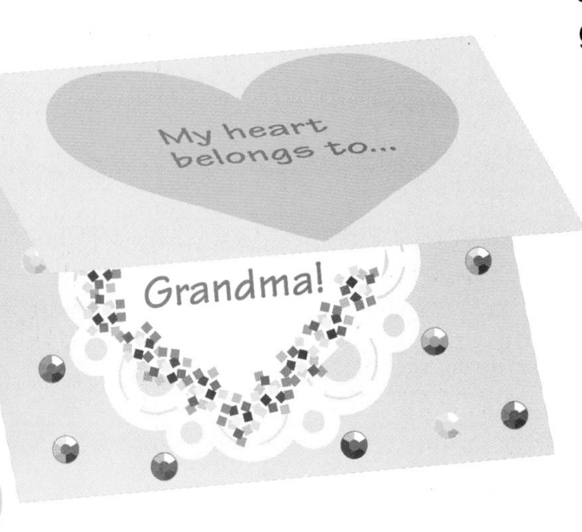

Colleen Dabney—Gr. 6, Williamsburg Christian Academy, Williamsburg, VA

Back-To-Nature Bookmarks

Get your students back to nature and into books with this unique art activity. Take your students for a nature walk and instruct each student to find four or five tiny leaves. If a nature walk is not practical for your location, have students draw and cut out four or five small leaf patterns. Then direct each student to follow the directions below to create his own back-to-nature bookmark.

Materials for each student:
newspaper
1 1/2" x 5 1/2" strip of Fun Foam™
collection of tiny leaves
Delta® Colormist spray
thin black or green marker
hole puncher
raffia

Directions for each student:

1. Cover your work area with newspaper.
2. Arrange the leaves on the strip of foam.
3. Carefully spray the foam strip and leaves with an even coating of Delta® Colormist. Let dry for about 15 minutes; then use a black or green marker to add details to each leaf.
4. Make a hole at the top of the strip using the hole puncher.
5. Insert the raffia and secure it with a knot.

Colleen Dabney—Gr. 6, Williamsburg Christian Academy, Williamsburg, VA

Reusable Pictograph Paper Dolls

Create eye-catching pictographs with this easy-to-use idea. During the first week of school, enlarge then duplicate the paper-doll pattern on page 94 for each student. Supply the student with a variety of art supplies—crayons, markers, glitter, yarn, fabric scraps, scissors, and glue. Instruct him to write his name along the length of the doll, then use the art supplies to decorate it. Collect each student's doll; then write the following categories on separate slips of construction paper: "Football," "Baseball," "Basketball," "Swimming," "Tennis," and "Other." Post each slip down the left-hand side of a bulletin board. Poll each student to find out which of the posted sports is his favorite. Then instruct the student to tape his paper doll beside his favorite sport. Inform the students that they've just created a pictograph. Hang on to the paper dolls after taking down the bulletin board and use them throughout the year to graph future class data.

Wanda McLaurin—Gr. 5, Bangert Elementary, New Bern, NC

A Picture Is Worth A Thousand Words

Invite your students to prove that a picture is worth a thousand words with the following activity. Give each student a 9" x 12" cutout of the first letter of her name. Supply the student with old magazines, markers, scissors, and glue. Instruct the student to find pictures that represent aspects of her personality, such as favorite sports, foods, hobbies, etc. Have the student cut out and glue the pictures collage-style to her letter. Encourage the student also to add original art to her letter. Direct each student to write her name on the back of her letter; then collect the letters and post them on a wall or bulletin board. Have each student try to figure out which letter belongs to which student. This can prove to be quite a challenge, since many students' names begin with the same letter.

Wanda McLaurin—Gr. 5, Bangert Elementary, New Bern, NC

Fall Frame Art

Channel your students' excitement about the season into this fanciful fall art activity! Give each student one 12" x 18" sheet of drawing paper, one 12" x 18" sheet of colored construction paper, one 2" x 2" square of tagboard, a pencil, a ruler, scissors, and crayons. Instruct each student to draw and color a fall-related picture on his sheet of drawing paper, leaving a two-inch border around the outer edges of his drawing. Then have each student draw a simple fall pattern such as a pumpkin on the tagboard square and cut it out. Have the student use a ruler to draw a two-inch-thick border around his colored sheet of construction paper. Instruct each student to place his tagboard pattern on the two-inch border, then use a pencil to outline the pattern at various angles, creating a continuous pattern around the border. Next have him cut out the decorative border, creating a frame for his fall drawing. Instruct the student to turn the cut-out frame over to hide the tracing marks, match the edges of the frame to the edges of his picture, and glue the frame in place.

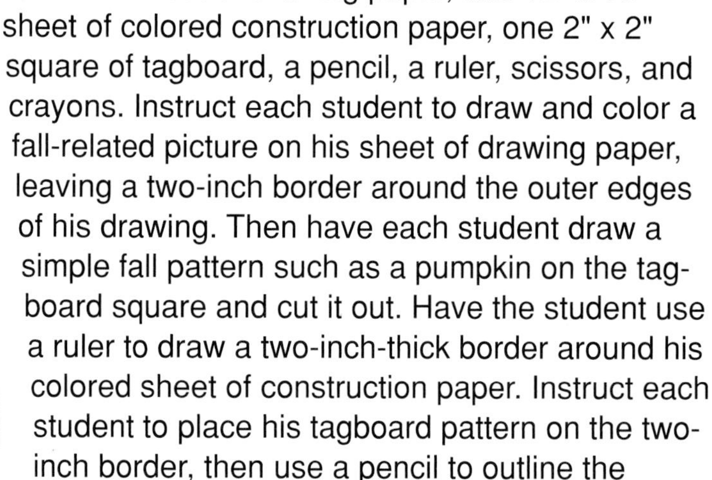

Tim Jones—Grs. 4–5, Cherrywood Acres School, Niagara Falls, Ontario, Canada

3-D Nametags

Get to know your students' interests as you learn their names by having them make personalized desktags. Give each student a piece of 12-inch-long oaktag. Instruct the student to fold the oaktag in half lengthwise. Then have the student write her name in large block letters that extend from the top to the bottom of the nametag. Direct the student to fill in the letters and the bottom of the nametag with decorative pictures about herself. Next have the student cut around the top half of each letter, then fold down the excess paper around each letter. Finally have the student place her personalized nametag on her desk.

J
jump rope

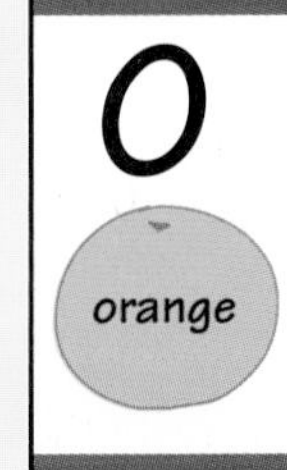

School Pride Quilt

Boost your students' school pride with the following art activity. Cut 26 8" x 8" squares of cotton muslin. Then cut 26 12" x 12" squares of different-colored felt. Give one cotton square and one felt square to each student. Assign each student a different letter of the alphabet. Instruct the student to use fabric markers to create symbols on the cotton square that begin with his assigned letter and are representative of the school. For example, a student assigned the letter *B* may draw a book, a band instrument, and a basketball. After each student's cotton square is decorated, have him glue it to the center of his felt square. Enlist a parent volunteer to sew the pieces of felt together in order, creating a quilt. Display the quilt in a hallway to show off your students' school pride.

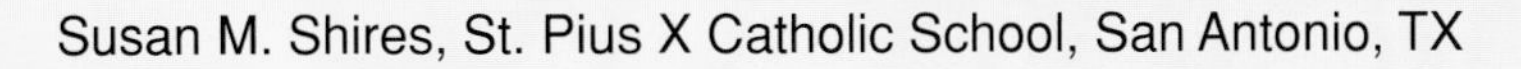
Susan M. Shires, St. Pius X Catholic School, San Antonio, TX

Biographical Boxes

Don't throw away those empty cereal boxes! Recycle the boxes by having students use them to make three-dimensional biographies. Assign each student a famous person to research. Instruct each student to write a brief biography of his famous person on a 5" x 8" index card. After the student has completed the brief biography, have him construct a model of his famous person. Give each student an empty cereal box, one Styrofoam® ball, and a supply of craft materials—construction paper, fabric scraps, felt, buttons, beads, yarn, glue, scissors, and markers. Then direct the student to use the various art supplies to create a body, arms, legs, clothing, and a head for his model. Assist the students in using a hot glue gun to attach the arms, legs, and Styrofoam® heads to their cereal boxes. After each student has created his model, direct him to glue his biographical information to the back of the model. Have students share their research; then display the models on a table or shelf.

Ellen M. Palmer, Meadowvale Elementary, Toledo, OH

Games

So...How Was School Today?

The end of the day can be quite hectic. Use this typically chaotic time to review the positives of the day. Each day select a different student from one group or table to make a statement about an activity he enjoyed, something he learned, or something positive that happened during the day. For example: "I enjoyed making pottery in art today," "Mary helped me practice my math facts," or "I learned in a science experiment that sound travels through water." Then allow the student and the other members of his group to get their backpacks. Repeat the process with each group. You will soon find that your students enjoy a less chaotic and more meaningful end of the day. Also, when a parent asks, "What did you do in school today?" he'll get a response other than "I don't know" or "Nothing."

Maureen Winkler—Gr. 5
Winter Springs Elementary, Winter Springs, FL

Beach-Ball Toss

Make use of any free time throughout the day to play a little catch with your students. Purchase a soft, bouncy ball—small beach balls work well—to keep handy at your desk. When you have a few minutes between activities, whip out the ball and ask the class a question about a current unit of study. Direct students who wish to answer the question to raise their hands. Call out the name of a student whose hand is up and toss the ball to that student. After the student answers the question, have him toss the ball back to you. If the student answers incorrectly, repeat the question and throw the ball to another student whose hand is raised. Repeat the process with several questions. Students will have such a ball answering questions they won't realize they've just had a lesson review!

Christine Snodgrass, Stephenson Elementary
Portland, OR

Tic-Tac-Toe Time Filler

Who doesn't love a good game of tic-tac-toe? Use this game as an end-of-lesson review. Make an overhead transparency of a tic-tac-toe grid. Divide your students into two teams: an *X* team and an *O* team. Begin by asking the *X* team a question. If the team answers the question correctly, allow a member to write an *X* in a square using an overhead projector pen. If the team doesn't answer the question correctly, ask the *O* team the same question. If the *O* team answers correctly, a member writes an *O* in a square; then the team gets its original turn. Play the game until one team gets three *X*s or three *O*s in a row. Then simply wipe off the transparency and you're ready for the next game!

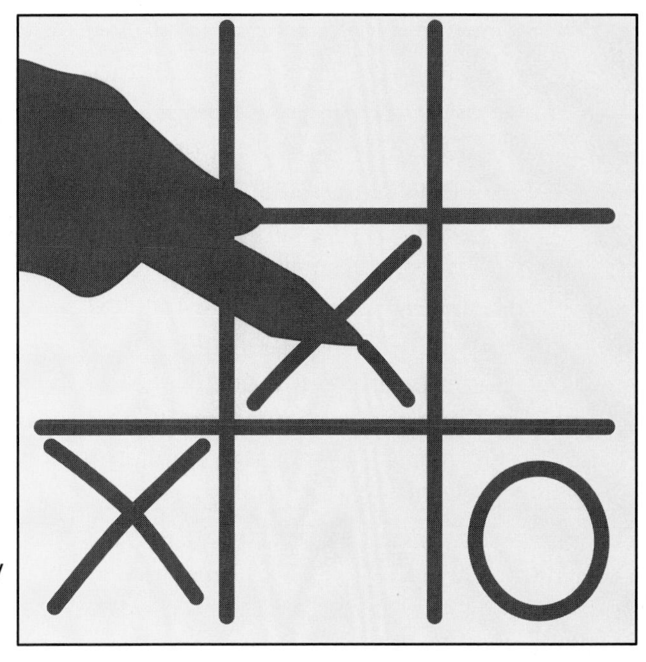

David Reitz—Gr. 4
Glenwood Elementary
Virginia Beach, VA

Eraser Chase

Here's a great rainy-day idea that gets your students up and moving around. Divide students into two teams. (Boys against girls is fun for this game!) Select a starting student from each team. Instruct the two students to stand at opposite ends of the classroom; then give each student a chalkboard eraser and tell him to balance it on top of his head. Designate one student as the "chaser" and the other as the "chasee." Say, "Go!" and let the chase begin. If the chaser tags the chasee, his team earns a point. If either student drops his eraser during the chase, the opposing team gets a point. Add a twist to the game by calling out, "Switch!" Upon hearing this, the chaser becomes the chasee and vice versa. Students will have a lot of fun and use up a lot of stored energy!

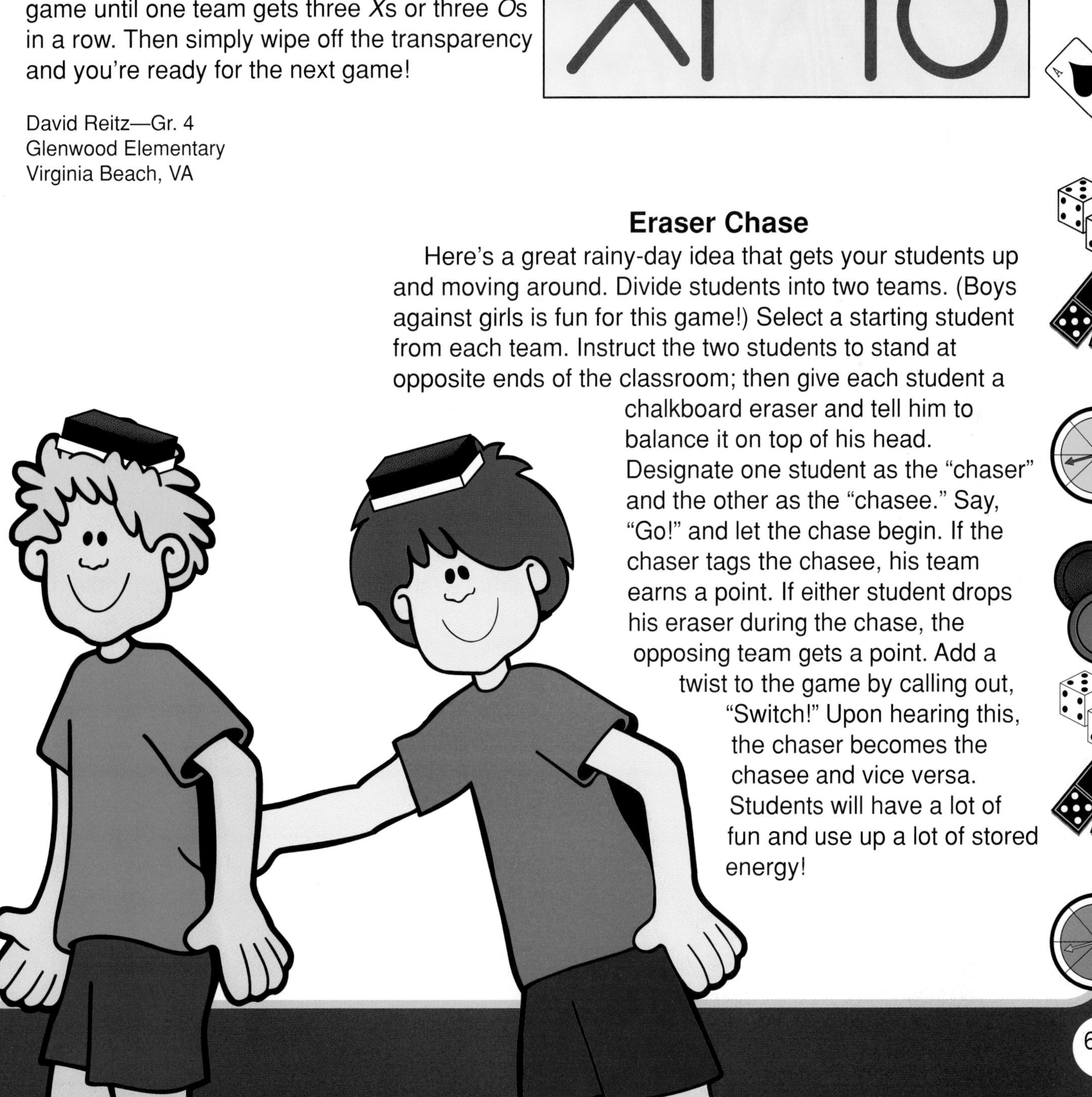

Who's Got A Secret?

Ease the first-day jitters with this secret-searching icebreaker. Before playing the game, direct each student to write down on an unsigned piece of paper one positive secret about herself that no one else in the classroom knows. Collect the papers and inform the students that their secrets will be used to play a game later in the day. Then divide an 8 1/2" x 11" sheet of paper into squares based on the number of students in your class. In each square write one student's secret; then duplicate a class supply. Distribute one copy to each student. Instruct each student to find out to whom each secret belongs by mingling and getting the owner of each secret to initial the appropriate square. Direct students to repeat this for each secret. Add a twist by challenging students to get initials in a diagonal, horizontal, or vertical line across the grid. Your class will easily get acquainted using this fun format.

Catherine A. Eighmy—Grs. 4–5
Moore Elementary, Fort Collins, CO

Numbers Rolled: 2 and 3

Toby ate two hot dogs at the fair. Each hot dog cost $1.50. Joe ate three times the amount of Toby. How many hot dogs did Joe eat and how much did they all cost?

Not Just A Roll Of The Dice

Practice makes perfect when it comes to mastering word problems. Why not make a game of it while giving your students the practice they need? Give each pair of students an index card. Next roll a pair of dice and call out the two numbers shown. (Make it more challenging by rolling three or four dice, adding zeros, or adding decimals.) Have each pair record the two numbers on its index card. Then instruct each pair to construct a word problem using the numbers. Have the pair solve its problem on back of the card. Award the pair one point if it correctly writes and solves its word problem. Collect the cards. Distribute a different card to each pair; then have the pair solve the new word problem on a piece of scrap paper. Give each pair a point for correctly solving the new problem. If time allows, repeat the process. Keep track of each pair's score and reward the first pair to reach 12 points.

Patricia Twohey—Gr. 4
Old Country Road School, Smithfield, RI

Arithmetic Aerobics

Strengthen basic facts and firm up those mental math skills with a game of Cerebral 21. The object of the game is for each student to draw a number card, then use any one of the four basic operations with the drawn card and a given total to make a number sentence equaling as close to 21 as possible. Create the number cards by writing the digits 1–10 on separate notecards. Then direct a student to draw two cards. Encourage the student to use any of the four basic operations and the two cards to create a number sentence with a solution as close to 21 as possible. (For example, 5 x 4 = 20 would be a possible number sentence for a student drawing a five card and a four card.) Award the student points equal to the difference between the sentence total and 21. Reshuffle the cards; then direct the next student to draw one number card. Instruct the student to use his card and the previous student's answer to construct a number sentence with a solution as close to 21 as possible. Repeat the process for each student. The student who ends the game with the least number of points wins the game.

Terry Healy—Gifted K–6, Eugene Field Elementary
Manhattan, KS

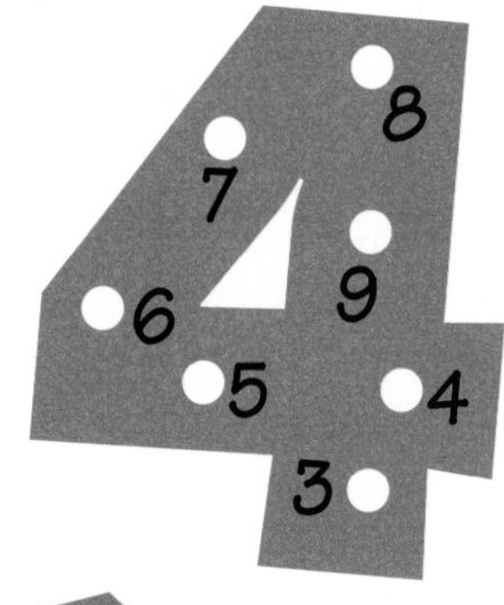

I've Got Your Number!

Help students get a handle on basic multiplication facts with this unique activity! Trace and cut out the numbers 0–12 from construction paper. Make duplicates so that each student has one cutout. On the front of each cutout, randomly write the numbers 0–12. Punch a hole near each number written on the cutout. Turn the cutout over. Next to each hole, write the product that would result from multiplying the cut-out number by the number recorded on the front next to the hole.

Give a number cutout to each student. Instruct the student to hold his cutout facing him and stick a pencil point through a numbered hole. Instruct the student to multiply this chosen number by the cut-out number. Have him check his answer by looking at the number beside the hole on the back of the cutout. Direct the student to do this for each digit on the cutout. Have students exchange cutouts when they're finished and repeat the process. Use this method to review division, addition, and subtraction facts, too.

David Reitz—Gr. 4, Glenwood Elementary, Virginia Beach, VA

Writing

Class Historians

Days come and go, and before you know it the end of another school year has arrived. Have your students keep track of the year by creating a class history. Before the first day of school, purchase a spiral notebook and label it "A Year To Remember." Stress to your students the importance of remembering each day. Inform the class that each student will be a class historian. At the end of each day, select a different student to make an entry in the book highlighting the day's events, such as what was studied, student birthdays, special guests, and special activities. Each week, invite a student to choose two or three entries from the prior week to illustrate. Your students will gradually discover that each day in itself is special, and you'll have a wonderful memento of the year.

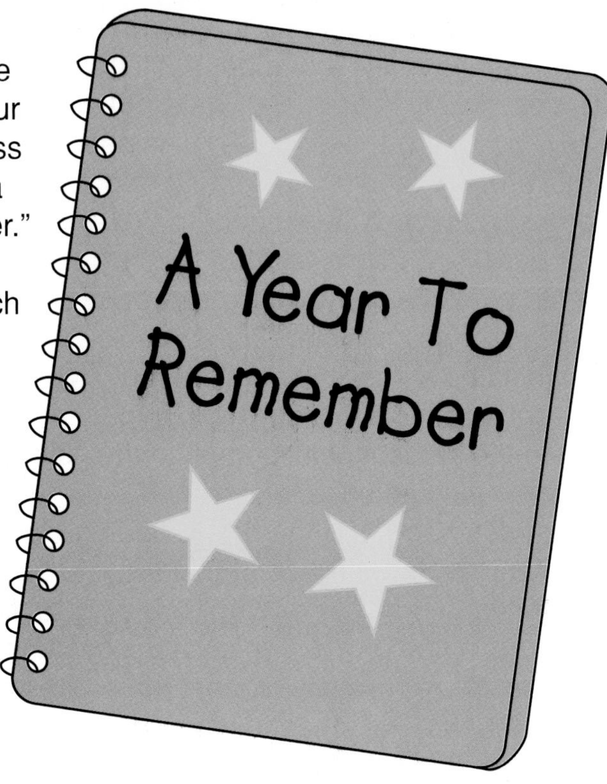

Julie Eick-Granchelli—Gr. 4
Towne Elementary
Medina, NY

The Year At A Glance

What could be easier than using a roll of adding-machine tape to create a timeline of class events? At the beginning of each week, cut off a 12-inch piece of adding-machine tape. Use a ruler and pencil to mark off a ten-inch horizontal line down the center of the tape; then divide the line into two-inch increments. Label each increment with a small vertical line, noting the day of the week and the date. Select a different student to be the class recorder for each week. Instruct the recorder to highlight at least one classroom event or activity for each day of the school week, such as birthdays, arrival of a new student, a field trip, or a special assembly. At the end of each week, post the tape on the wall just below the ceiling, creating a continuous timeline around the room. Use the timeline during parent conferences to quickly update parents on classroom activities.

Julie Eick-Granchelli

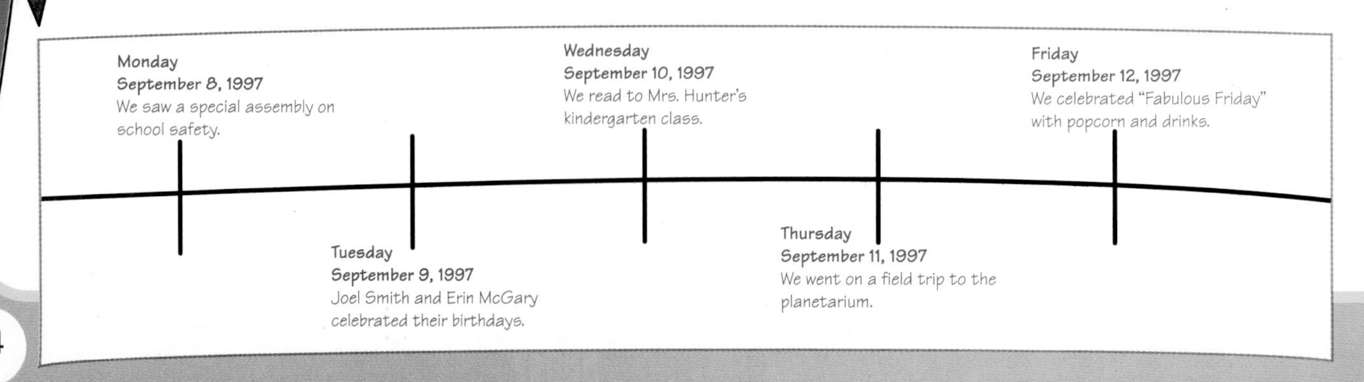

Showcase Of The Stars

We all know that each student is unique in his own way. Help each student let his light shine with the following activity. Duplicate a class supply of page 95 on yellow construction paper; then distribute one to each student. Discuss with your class the importance of individuality and self-expression. Then direct each student to fill in every section of his star by completing each starter sentence and adding an illustration that expresses his uniqueness. Have each student cut out his star; then display it on a wall or bulletin board titled "Showcase Of The Stars."

Patricia Twohey—Gr. 4
Old County Road School
Smithfield, RI

Eye Spy

Teachers are experts at acknowledging positive student behaviors. Encourage your students to acknowledge positive behavior in their peers with this activity. Anytime throughout the day, call out, "Eye spy." At this point direct each student to take out her journal and write an entry acknowledging the positive behavior of a fellow classmate. At the end of three or four minutes, call out, "Eye spy" again to signal students to stop writing. Then have each student read her entry to the rest of the class. You'll find your students not only recognizing positive behaviors, but modeling them as well.

Barbara Samuels—Gr. 5
Riverview School
Denville, NJ

Greatest Hits

Tune into your students and turn on their creativity with this activity! Create a student handout containing a large, blank television screen. Duplicate a class supply of the handout and distribute one to each student. Instruct the student to write a short synopsis of his life as if it were a television show. Have the student include highlights such as when and where he was born, where he has lived, who's in his family, and how he spends his time. Then have the student illustrate and color one scene from his life on the blank television screen. Display each student's illustration and synopsis on a wall or bulletin board titled "Our Greatest Hits."

Terry Healy—Gifted K–6
Eugene Field Elementary
Manhattan, KS

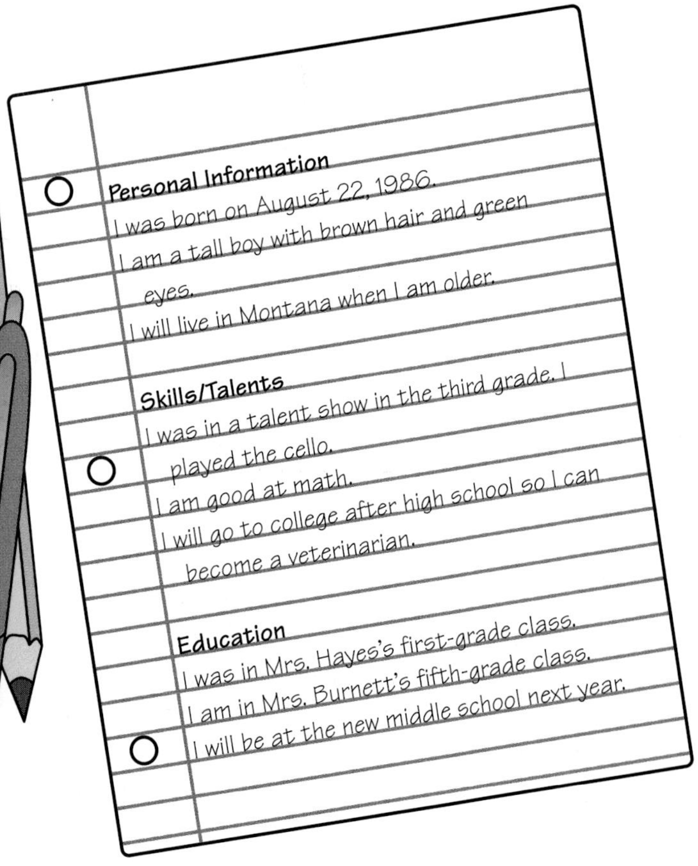

The Times Of Our Lives

Learn a little something about your students while helping them identify the past, present, and future. Discuss with students the differences between the three verb tenses—*past, present, future.* Then put the following sentence starters on the board: "I was…," "I am…," and "I will…." Have students reflect on their lives. Then ask each student: "How would you describe yourself today?", "How were you different in the past?", and "How will you be different in the future?" Next write various categories on the board such as personal information, skills/talents, education, and travel. Instruct each student to choose three of the categories listed and write a past, present, and future sentence about himself for each category chosen. Direct each student to put his name on the back of his list. Post each student's sentences on a wall or bulletin board titled "The Times Of Our Lives." Then have each student try to determine who each set of sentences is describing. Your students will have a handle on tense in no time.

Terry Healy

What I Didn't Do On My Summer Vacation

Get the creative juices flowing with this fun and unusual back-to-school writing assignment! Instead of asking students to write the usual paragraph describing what they did on their summer vacations, direct students to think about the things they didn't do on their summer vacations. As a class, brainstorm events such as white-water rafting down the Colorado River, swimming with dolphins, or going on a safari in Africa. Then instruct each student to write a paragraph titled "What I Didn't Do On My Summer Vacation." Encourage each student to be creative and include descriptions associated with his five senses to detail each event. Have each student share his writing with the class; then post each student's paragraph for all to enjoy. Be prepared to experience a positive first-writing activity with your students as well as a few laughs!

Barbara Samuels—Gr. 5, Riverview School, Denville, NJ

It's A Sign!

Are you looking for something to help you keep track of your students at each phase of the writing process? Post the following signs on your chalkboard during your Writer's Workshop time: "Writer's Workshop In Progress," "Need To See An Editor," "Editors On Duty," and "Author's Chair Readers." As each student finishes a rough draft, direct her to sign her name under the sign that reads "Need To See An Editor." When student editors are ready to help their classmates, have them sign their names under the "Editors On Duty" sign. Instruct students who are ready to share their work with the class to write their names under the sign labeled "Author's Chair Readers." This easy process will keep you and your students moving in the right direction.

Karen Arnett, Chesapeake, VA

TECHNOLOGY

Opening Eyes To The Future

Take advantage of your school's open-house program to familiarize parents and the community with your instructional technology program. Give hands-on demonstrations of ways instructional technology is being integrated into the curriculum. Demonstrate new software and equipment, and allow parents to explore with their children. Set up computers to facilitate on-line searches, desktop publishing, and the use of multimedia resources. What a great way to expose parents and students to the latest technology your school has to offer!

Andrea Troisi—Librarian, LaSalle Middle School, Niagara Falls, NY

Summer Reading

Need an easy, nonthreatening way to get students using your class computer at the beginning of the year? Have each student think about the books he read during the summer and what he was doing while he read them. Then direct each student to type and complete the following sentence on the computer: "This summer I read ________ while ______________." Encourage the student to add clip art or use a drawing and painting software program to illustrate his sentence. Display each student's sentence on a wall in your classroom, library, or school media center.

Meg Turner—Gr. 5, Seawell Elementary, Chapel Hill, NC

R-E-S-P-E-C-T!

Tired of students abusing computer equipment? Teach your students to respect computer equipment from day one with the following idea. Have students brainstorm a list of computer "Do's" and "Don'ts." Record students' suggestions on the board. Be sure to include your own suggestions in the list. Have students select the top ten "Do's" and "Don'ts" from the class list. Record these guidelines on a chart and post it near the computer station in your classroom. Then create a computer contract for each student to sign, pledging he will observe the guidelines established by the class. With the help of this advance planning, your equipment will fare much better in the long run!

Meg Turner

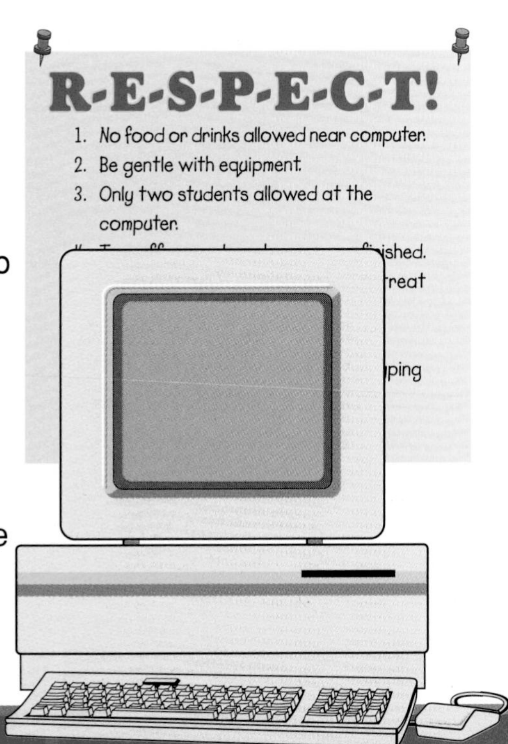

Lights, Camera, Action!

Instead of giving a lecture on "How To Use The Camcorder," why not team up with a few teachers to create an instructional video that will introduce video terms, parts, and operating instructions? Also outline for students the steps involved in creating a video—conceptualization, storyboards, scripts, rehearsals, sound, editing. Show the instructional video to the class as a whole; then set it up in a learning center. Quiz students on the proper video terms and techniques before allowing them to work in small groups to prepare their own video productions. You're sure to get some award-winning results!

Meg Turner—Gr. 5, Seawell Elementary, Chapel Hill, NC

Presentations With Pizzazz

Perk up your next lesson with the help of a multimedia presentation. Use software programs such as HyperCard®, HyperStudio™, and SuperCard® to make a series of slides relating to the topic or concept you plan to cover. Then record sound clips or narration to accompany your slides. Show the computer slide-show presentation as an introduction to the unit. Afterwards, set up the presentation on a computer for independent student interaction and reinforcement. Your students will become familiar with the content while learning exciting multimedia techniques!

Meg Turner

Mining The Internet

The ideas and suggestions of fellow teachers often prove to be worth their weight in gold. Access the Internet and network with other educators across the globe to cash in on the wealth of information that exists among your peers. Join a listserv to link up with other educators for an information exchange or simply get on-line and chat. To begin, complete a search on education-related web sites using your Internet browser's search engine. Then sit back and get ready to be amazed by the number of educational resources you will find. For more information on how to access and use the Internet in your classroom, read *Internet For Kids: A Beginner's Guide To Surfing The Net* by Ted Pedersen and Francis Moss (Price Stern, 1995).

Patricia Altman—Gr. 6, Lewis M. Klein Middle School, Harrison, NY

Keying Into Technology

"How do I save on my disk?" "What's a document?" "How do I print?" Do these questions sound familiar? To help students answer many of their own questions, create a technology handbook providing simple directions on everything from turning on the computer, to formatting a disk or logging onto the network. Offer minisessions to students who need extra instruction. Organize a mentor program that pairs novice computer users with more experienced users in your classroom. What a great way to capitalize on existing resources within your classroom and get everyone up to speed on the latest technology!

Andrea Troisi—Librarian, LaSalle Middle School, Niagara Falls, NY

Jovial
Astonishing
Kind
Energetic

Computer Formatting

Looking for a fun way to teach your students about the formatting capabilities of your computer? Have each student use the word-processing program on your classroom computer to make an acrostic poem of his name. Instruct each student to type his name in a vertical column. Direct the student to use a dictionary or thesaurus to come up with one self-describing adjective for each letter in his name. Instruct the student to type each word beside the appropriate letter in his name. Show students how to use the mouse and blinking cursor to highlight areas of text and experiment with different fonts and styles for each adjective. Instruct each student to print his poem; then display the poems for others to enjoy.

Meg Turner—Gr. 5
Seawell Elementary, Chapel Hill, NC

Computer Learning Centers

Looking for a challenging learning center that will utilize your computer? If so, try this great idea! Make a list of current and past topics covered in class—science, math, social studies, and health topics work well. Have each student choose a topic on which to write an informational booklet using the classroom computer and available word-processing and graphics software. Write the following list of essential book parts on an index card: Title page, Table of contents, Definitions, Illustrations, Graphs, Tables, Summary. Laminate the card and place it in the center. Require that each student's book contain clip art, graphs, and other color graphics. Instruct each student to print his booklet, then use brads or a stapler to bind his book. Use the booklets during conference time to show parents topics covered in class, as well as an example of how students are using technology in the classroom.

Meg Turner

We're All Stars!

Here's a great way to keep waiting parents entertained on conference day. Videotape your students, highlighting the events of the first grading period. Assign each student a specific duty in producing the video. At the end of the highlights, videotape a personalized message from each student. Before conferences begin, set up a television, VCR, and several chairs in the hall outside your classroom. Post directions for viewing the video on top of the television. Parents will appreciate and enjoy this student-made video.

Pam Chemelewski—Gr. 5, Robert Lee Frost, IPS #106, Indianapolis, IN

Rejuvenate Those Reproducibles!

Put a new spin on reproducibles with this creative idea! Capitalize on your classroom computer's capabilities by creating several templates, associated with a unit of study, for students to complete on the computer. Assign each template a specific file name; then save an additional backup of each template on a floppy disk in case a student accidentally alters the original template. List questions and problems for students to answer on each template. Teach each student how to save his responses on his data disk to avoid altering the master template. When you want to reinforce a concept, instruct a student to open a specific file and complete the enclosed activity. Direct the student to print a hard copy of his work and turn it in so you can assess his work.

Meg Turner—Gr. 5, Seawell Elementary, Chapel Hill, NC

Let's Get Started

One of the most difficult aspects of managing a single-computer classroom is allocating time for everyone to use the computer. Solve this dilemma by taking advantage of your computer during quiet activity periods throughout the day such as journal-writing and silent-reading periods. Allow two students to pair up and work on the computer during these periods. Use the computer to make a schedule and assign each student pair a specific computer time. Have the two assigned students work on basic computer operating techniques at first, eventually progressing to more difficult programs and tasks. What a great way to maximize computer usage in your room!

	M	T	W	Th	F
Silent Reading	Evan Adrienne	Earl Matt	Nick Alex	Mike Cory	Bill R.J.
Journal Writing	Alana Melody	Maddie Greg	Kailie Sarah	Debra Liz	Jim Ray
End-Of-Day	Eddie Chris	Sharon Ruby	Andrew Don	Keith Don	Carol Mary

Meg Turner

Literature

Talking It Up!

Looking for an alternative to the traditional paper-and-pencil book report? Once a month have each student prepare an oral presentation or book talk on a novel she recently has read. Provide each student with a copy of the graphic organizer on page 96 to use in preparing and presenting her book talk. Discuss each section of the organizer with the students; then direct each student to also include in her book talk a visual aid such as using a prop or poster, or dressing as a major character. What a great way to help students develop oral communication skills while drawing attention to great literature!

Gwen Burnett—Gr. 5, Seawell Elementary, Chapel Hill, NC

Now Featuring...

Bring literature to life by honoring a different author each month. Display pictures and personal information about the selected author on a bulletin board. Gather several copies of the author's books for students to read during the month. Locate the address of the author and have students write a friendly letter to her discussing her work. Students will be motivated to read when they learn about the interesting lives of their favorite authors.

Maureen Winkler

Sept. 8, 1997

Dear Mrs. Lowry,

I really enjoyed your book <u>Number The Stars</u>. It made me cry. You write as though you were right there. Your description of the scene with the broken necklace was really good. I was scared too for what would happen next. Thank you for writing such a good book. I look forward to reading other books that you have written.

Sincerely,
Tressa DiGiorgio

Time-Capsule Book Reports

Follow up the reading of your next novel by assigning this creative book report. Discuss the purpose of time capsules with your students. Invite student volunteers to bring in objects for a class time capsule to be opened at the end of the year. Then have each student create his own literature time capsule from a shoebox. Instruct each student to record the title, author, and a brief summary of events on the exterior of the box. Encourage each student to add appropriate illustrations to the exterior of his box. Then direct each student to put five objects related to the book in his time capsule. Have each student discuss the significance of each item in his time capsule to the rest of the class. You'll never find a more timely book report!

Maureen Winkler—Gr. 5, Winter Springs Elementary, Winter Springs, FL

Newsworthy Books

Get the scoop on the books your students read with this creative book-report format! Have each student use a newspaper format to report on a book. Direct each student to include brief articles on the plot, the author, and the main characters of the story. Instruct the student to write an editorial featuring his opinion of the book. Remind the student to include pictures of the main characters and of important events. Finally, direct each student to include a weather report for the area in which the story occurs. Display the finished newspapers/book reports on a bulletin board titled "Extra, Extra, Read All About It!" This is one book-report idea that's definitely hot off the presses!

Maureen Winkler—Gr. 5, Winter Springs Elementary, Winter Springs, FL

Nasty Or Nice: Students' Choice

Looking for a fun way to explain your discipline procedures at the beginning of the school year? Read aloud to your class *The Teacher From The Black Lagoon* by Mike Thaler (Scholastic Inc., 1989). Then explain to your students that their actions will determine whether they'll have the villainous Mrs. Green or the beautiful, caring Mrs. Green for a teacher. Point out that listening carefully, following directions, and putting forth their best efforts will ensure a teacher like the kind and generous Mrs. Green. Then explain your classroom rules and have your students discuss the importance of each rule.

Jill Barger—Gr. 4
Glenwood Elementary, Virginia Beach, VA

Putting First-Day Worries To Rest

Even veteran teachers suffer from the first-day jitters! Put those worries to rest with the help of the poem "Fifteen, Maybe Sixteen, Things To Worry About" from the book *If I Were In Charge Of The World* by Judith Viorst (Simon and Schuster Children's Books, 1984). Read the poem aloud to your students, discussing each worry outlined and the reasons behind it. Then have each student write a poem about his worries and concerns for the new school year. Students will feel much more at ease knowing they are not alone in their concerns.

Patricia Altman—Gr. 6, Lewis M. Klein Middle School, Harrison, NY

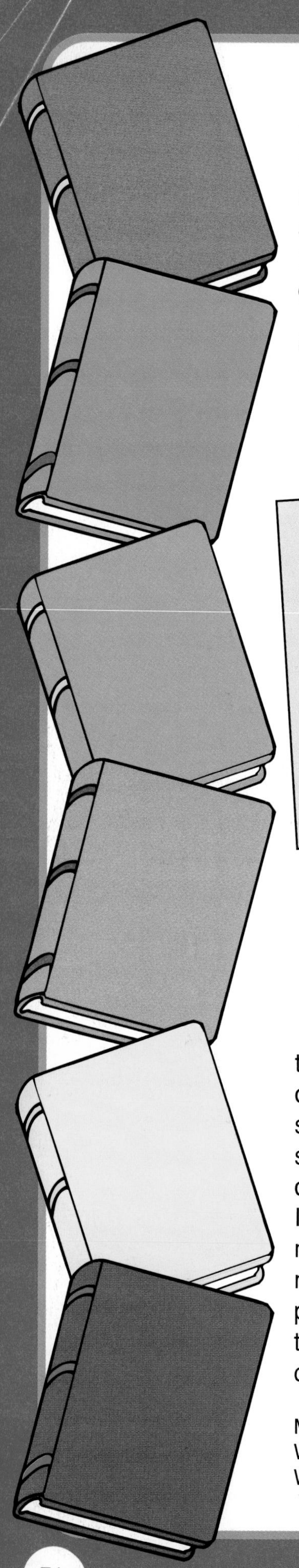

A New Year Doesn't Frighten Us

Looking for a way to ease your students' fears on the first day of school? Read *Life Doesn't Frighten Me* by Maya Angelou (Stewart, Tabori & Chang, Inc.; 1993), a poem in book form. Then ask each student to create his own booklet revealing his fears about the grade he has just entered. Direct the student to describe each fear in one short sentence, like Maya Angelou does in her poem, and include an illustration for each sentence. This activity is a great way to reveal and address the students' fears of the new school year!

Maxine Pincott—Gr. 4, Oliver Ellsworth School, Windsor, CT

We're Going Places!

My Goals

1. Make honor roll.
2. Learn to tap dance.
3. Turn homework in on time.

Kenny

Each school year signals the start of a new and unique journey for students and teachers. Start the year off on the right foot by reading the picture book *Oh, The Places You'll Go!* by Dr. Seuss (Random House Books For Young Readers, 1993). After reading the book, have each student write a letter to herself outlining what she hopes to accomplish during the upcoming year. Collect the letters and store them in a safe place; then return them at the end of the school year. Students will enjoy reflecting upon the places they've been and seeing which goals they have met.

Patricia Altman—Gr. 6, Lewis M. Klein Middle School, Harrison, NY

Postcard Report

Make reporting on books fun with this creative book-report format! Begin the activity by having each student read a fiction book of her choice. Then direct the student to design a postcard representing the book by drawing a scene from the story on the front of the postcard. On the back, have each student write a summary of the novel in the upper left-hand corner and draw a stamp featuring a main character in the upper right-hand corner. Instruct each student to address the postcard to the main character using a made-up address appropriate for the novel. Laminate the finished postcards; then bind them together to make a large booklet for your class to enjoy throughout the year!

Maureen Winkler—Gr. 5
Winter Springs Elementary
Winter Springs, FL

Reading All Around Us!

Five minutes is all you need to get your students thinking about reading. Divide your class into groups of three. Challenge each group to list as many items as it can think of that can be read. Encourage students to think of things they read during the course of a normal day such as textbooks, cereal boxes, magazines, letters, and computer screens. Invite each group to read its list to the rest of the class. Record the responses on a poster entitled "Reading Is Everywhere." Keep adding items to the list throughout the year.

Reading All Around Us!

- cereal box
- textbook
- map
- globe
- medicine bottle
- magazine
- computer screen
- newspaper

Patricia Twohey—Gr. 4
Old Country Road School
Smithfield, RI

Totally Awesome Books

T.A.B., or Totally Awesome Books, is a great way to incorporate independent reading into your classroom routine! Challenge each student to read 20 books by the end of the school year. When a student reads a book, instruct him to fill out an index card with basic information about the book—title, author, summary, critique, student's name, and date. Keep a file box on your desk with a section labeled for each student. When a student completes an index card, instruct him to file it in the box. Next post a small incentive chart on each student's desk. Check each student's file once a week and award him an incentive sticker for each new index card. Have a short conference with each student once a month to discuss the books he has read. After a student has read 20 books, present him with a T.A.B. award—a certificate of your design—and an incentive such as a free book or bookmark. If each student reaches his goal by the end of the year, hold a T.A.B. pizza party to celebrate. What a great way to get students reading!

Charting A Course For Reading

Set sail for a great year of reading with this easy-to-follow literature plan! Assign a different genre of literature for each month of the school year. Design a handout to send home with students showing the genres selected for the year. Suggested genres include: realistic fiction, mystery, adventure, science fiction, fantasy, historical fiction, sports fiction, nonfiction, and biography. Your students will enjoy smooth sailing while knowing well in advance the upcoming genres!

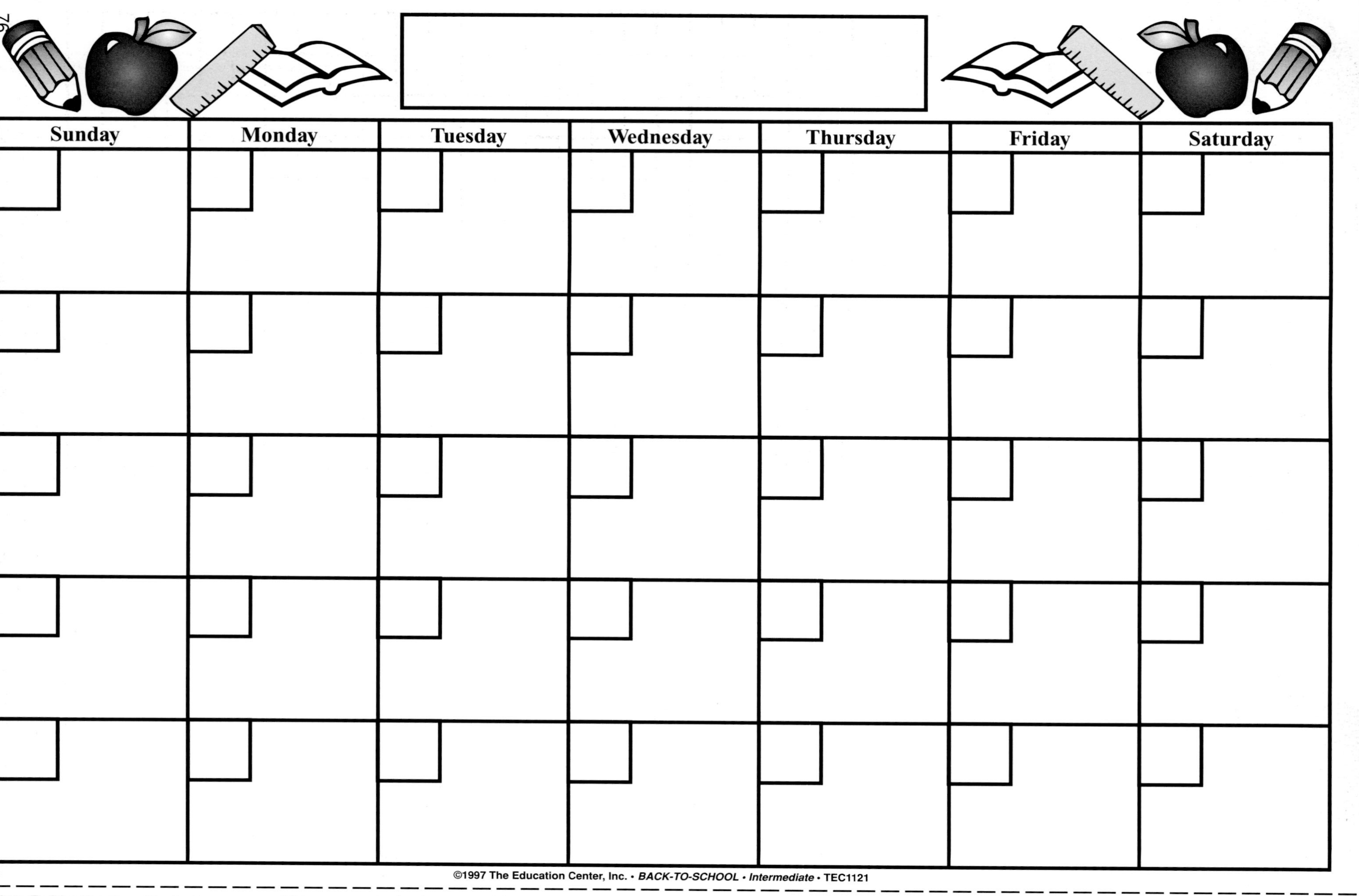

Note To The Teacher: Duplicate one copy of this page and write the name of the desired month in the box at the top of the calendar. Write the appropriate dates in the smaller squares underneath each day of the week. Use this open calendar for monthly planning or to keep parents informed of classroom activities.

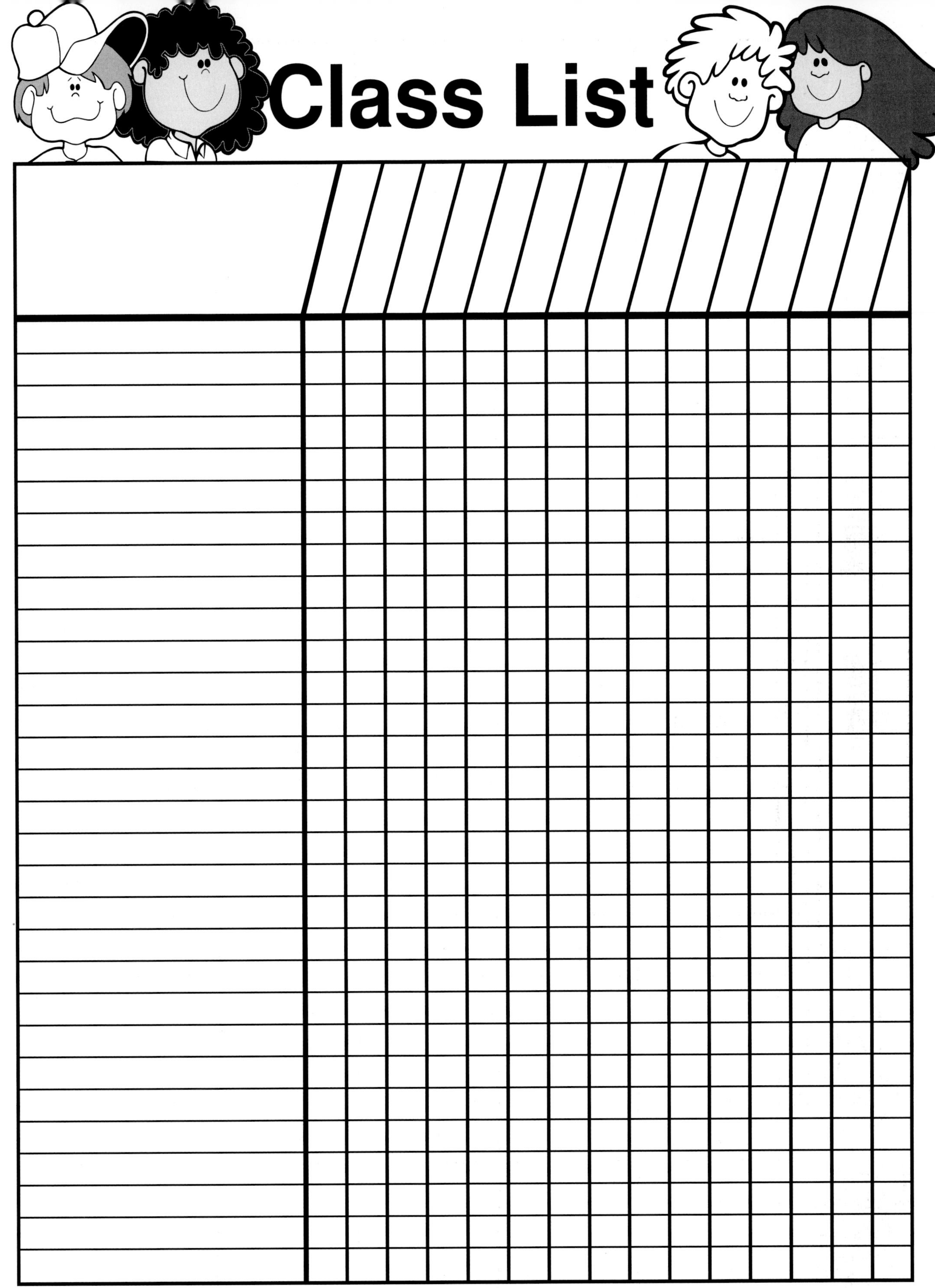

Note To The Teacher: Duplicate one copy of this page; then fill in the names of your students in alphabetical order along the left-hand column. Make multiple copies of your class list to keep track of grades, field-trip permission slips, fund-raisers, and various other activities.

Student Information Card

First name   Last name

Student No.

Address

City   State   Zip   Home phone

Mother's name   Father's name   Guardian's name

Mother's work phone   Father's work phone   Guardian's work phone

Student lives with mother ☐, father ☐, both parents ☐, guardian ☐.

In an emergency call: ____________ at ____________

Student's birth date: ____________

Comments: ____________

Good–Work Coupon

This coupon is good for

Name   Teacher

Good–Work Coupon

This coupon is good for

Name   Teacher

Class Coupon

Redeem this coupon for

Name   Teacher

Class Coupon

Redeem this coupon for

Name   Teacher

Note To The Teacher: Duplicate one copy of the "Student Information Card" to send home with each student. Instruct parents to complete the form and return it. Duplicate a class supply of the coupons to use as rewards and incentives.

School Supplies

Dear Parent,

______________________ needs

the following school supplies:

____ pencils ❑ No. 2 ❑ red

____ pens ❑ black ❑ blue ❑ red

____ markers ❑ all colors ❑ ____________

____ colored pencils

____ crayons

____ notebook paper ❑ wide ruled ❑ college ruled

____ 3-ring notebook(s)

____ spiral notebook(s) with ________ pages

____ folder(s) ❑ with pockets ❑ with brads

____ other: ______________________

____

____

Thank you,

____
teacher signature

____
date

Missed Assignments

Dear Parent,

______________________ needs to

complete the following assignments:

____

____

____

____

____

The work is due by ______________________ .

Your help and support are greatly appreciated.

WANTED:

Homework

Sincerely,

____
teacher signature

____
parent signature

Please sign and return.

Dear Parent,

Your conference for ______________________

has been scheduled at ______________________

on ______________________ , ______________________ .

Please complete the bottom portion of this form and return it to me as soon as possible.
I look forward to visiting with you.

Sincerely,

____
teacher signature

- -

❑ I plan to attend my child's conference at the scheduled time.

❑ I will need to reschedule our conference.

______________________ child's name

______________________ parent signature

Teacher Assistant Request

______________ M T W T F ______________
Date Time

To: ______________________

From: ______________________

Concerning: ______________________

Please

❑ call ______________________ about ______________________ .
phone number

❑ send to ______________________ .

❑ make copies. No. of copies: __________ ❑ one side ❑ both sides

❑ type.

❑ make a ditto or thermofax master.

❑ make a transparency.

❑ other ______________________

Comments: ______________________

____

Thanks!

Use with "Here's The Scoop" on page 4.

Name ____________ Getting-acquainted activity

Autographs, Please!

I slept in a tent.	I hiked a mile or more.	I acted in or attended a play.	I read a map.	I went to a party.
I slept over at a friend's house.	I celebrated my birthday.	I went on a trip.	I went to a museum.	I planted a garden.
I wrote a story or poem.	I went out to eat.	I ate an ice-cream sundae.	I made a new friend.	I went swimming.
I went to a fair or carnival.	I marched in or watched a parade.	I read a great book.	I went to a movie.	I stayed up really late.
I went to a zoo or park.	I went on a picnic.	I went to or played in a sports event.	I made something artistic.	I learned something cool.

Note To The Teacher: Duplicate a class supply of this page to use with "Autographs, Please!" on page 8.

Patterns

Use with "Sink Your Teeth Into A Cool School Year!" on page 22.

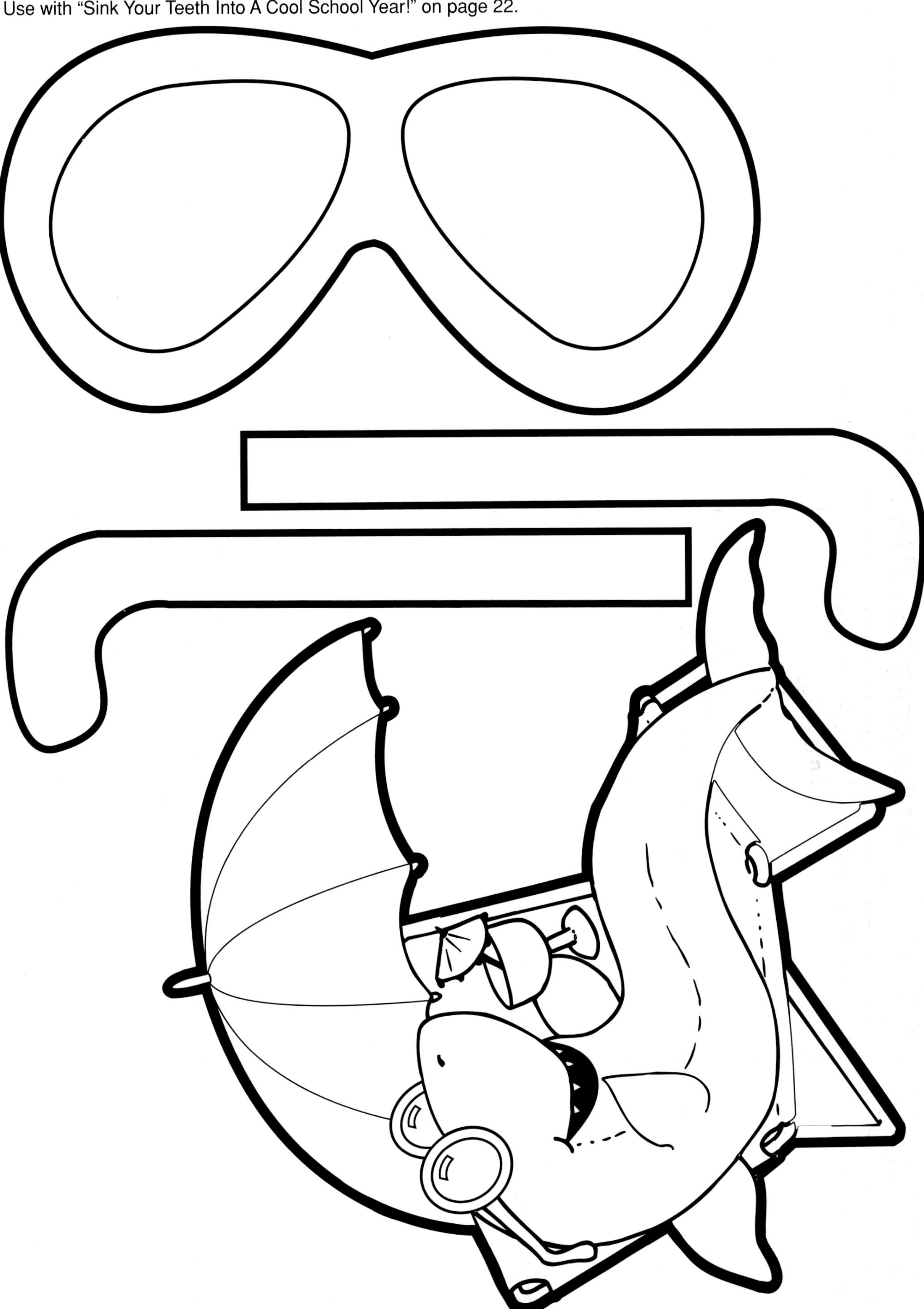

Pattern

Use with "Hats Off To A Great Group!" on page 22.

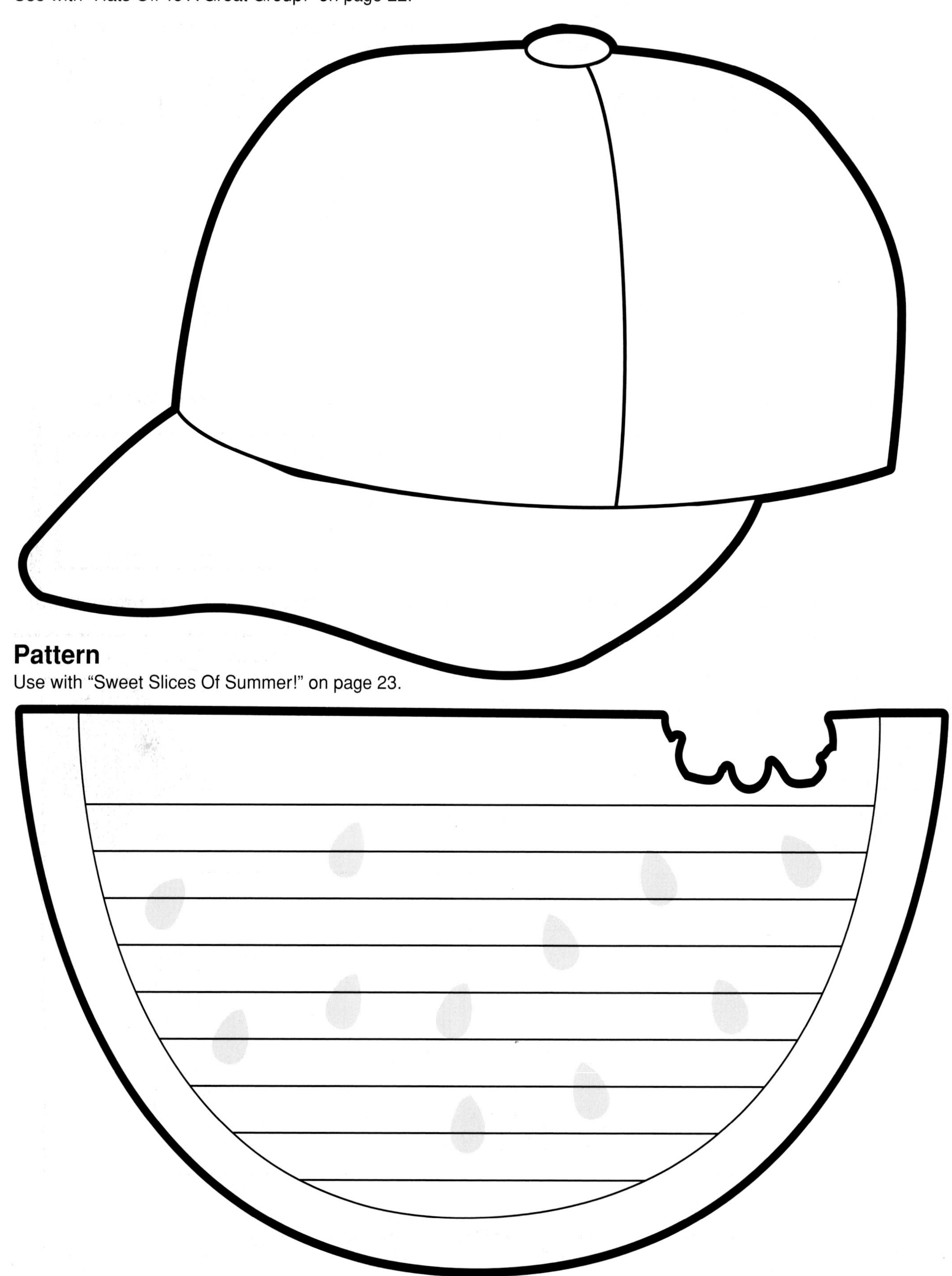

Pattern

Use with "Sweet Slices Of Summer!" on page 23.

Use with "Caution—Kids At Work!" on page 23.

ONE WAY

Use with "Presenting" on page 24.

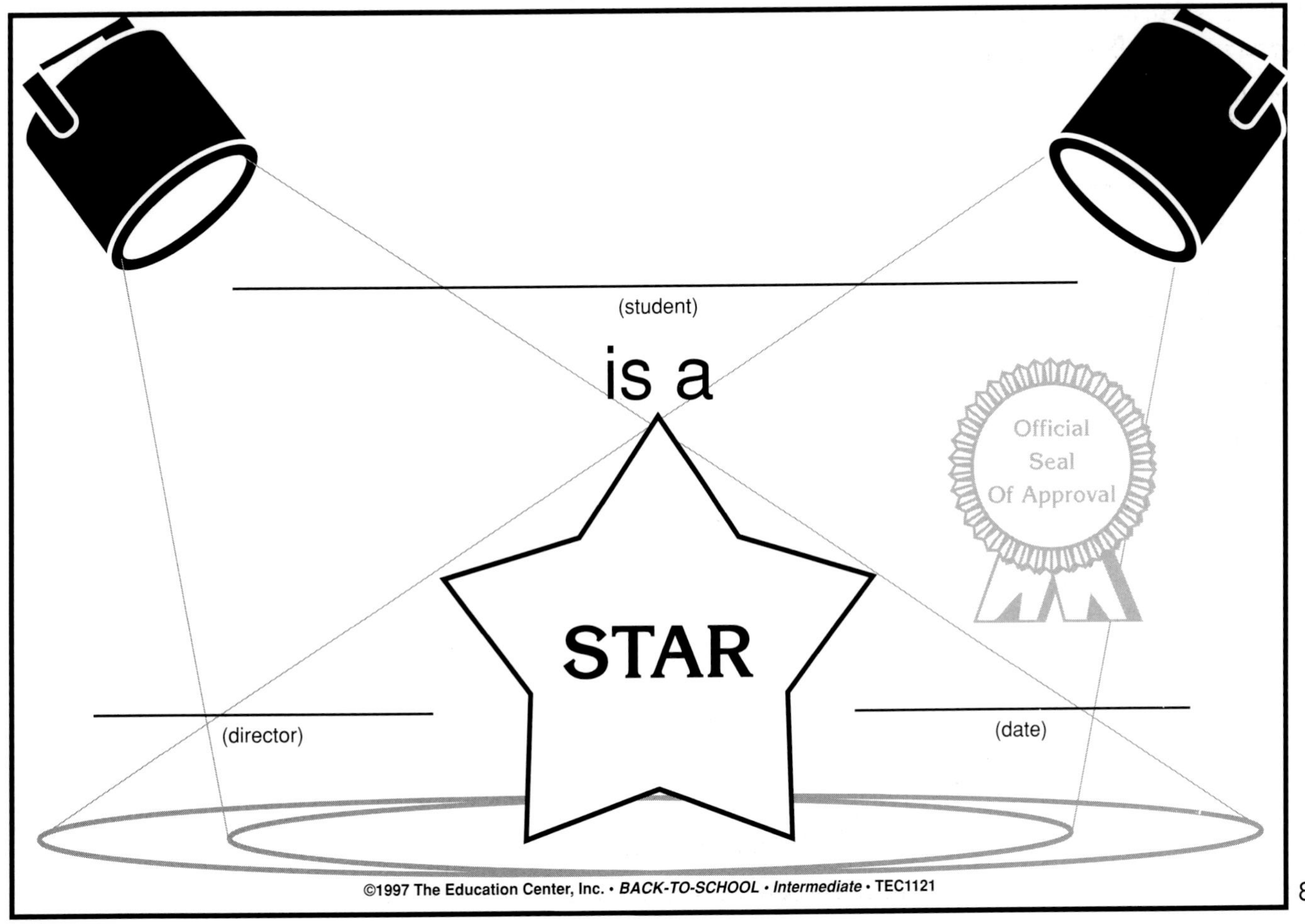

Patterns

Use with "Tools For Success" on page 24.

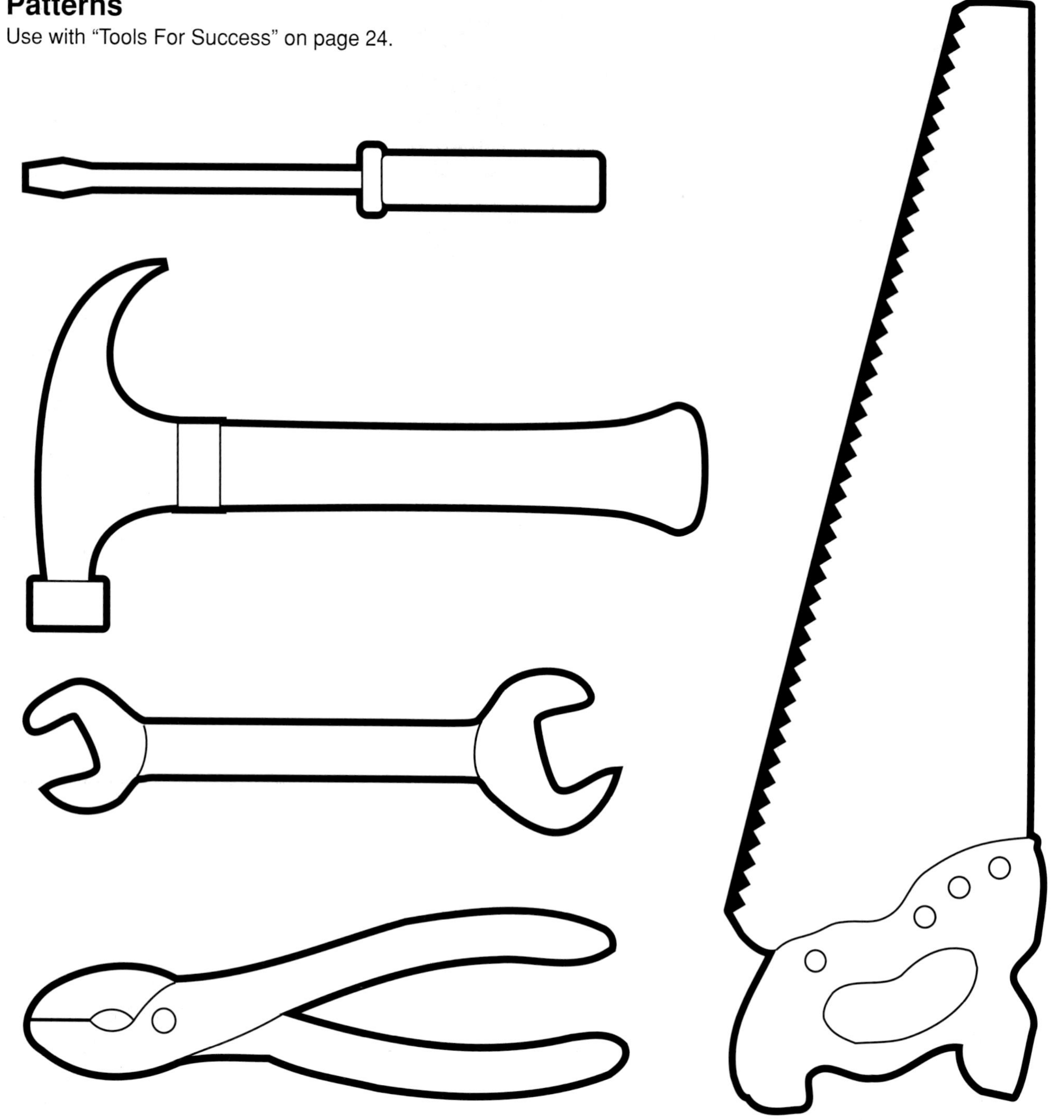

Use with "Fifth Graders Are A Sharp Bunch!" on page 25.

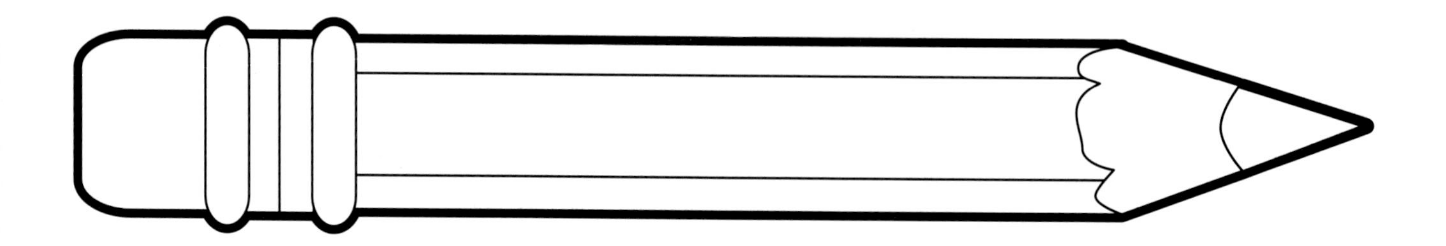

Use with "Reaching New Heights" on page 25.

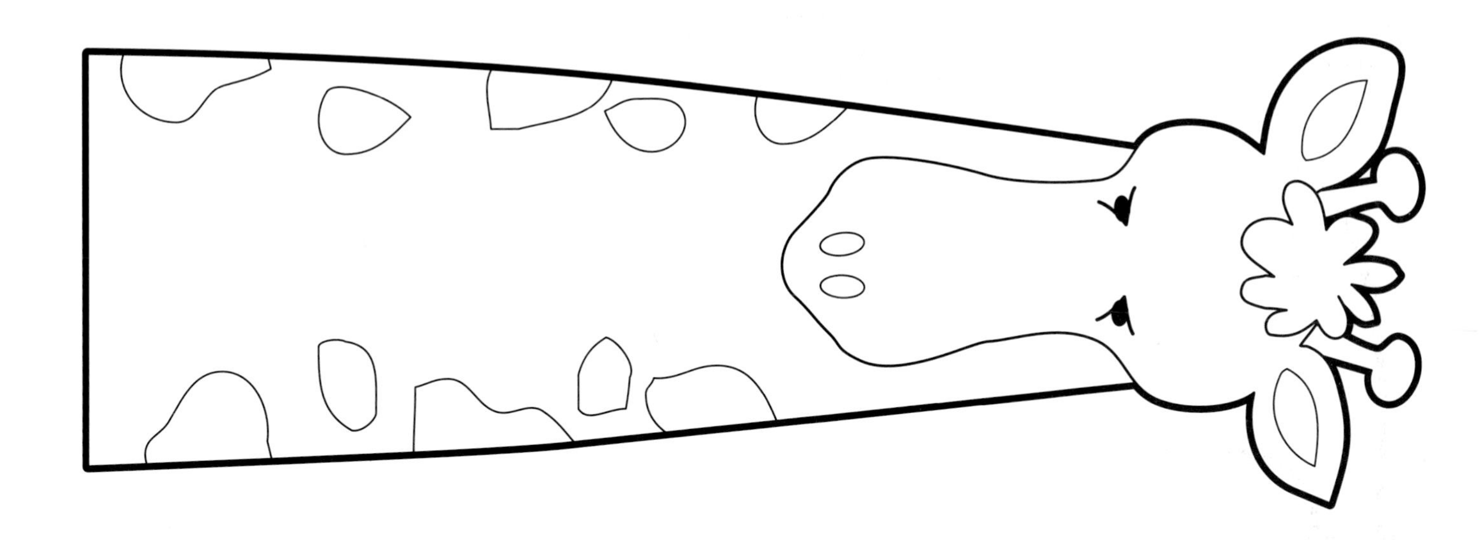

Use with "Our Game Plan For A Great Year!" on page 26.

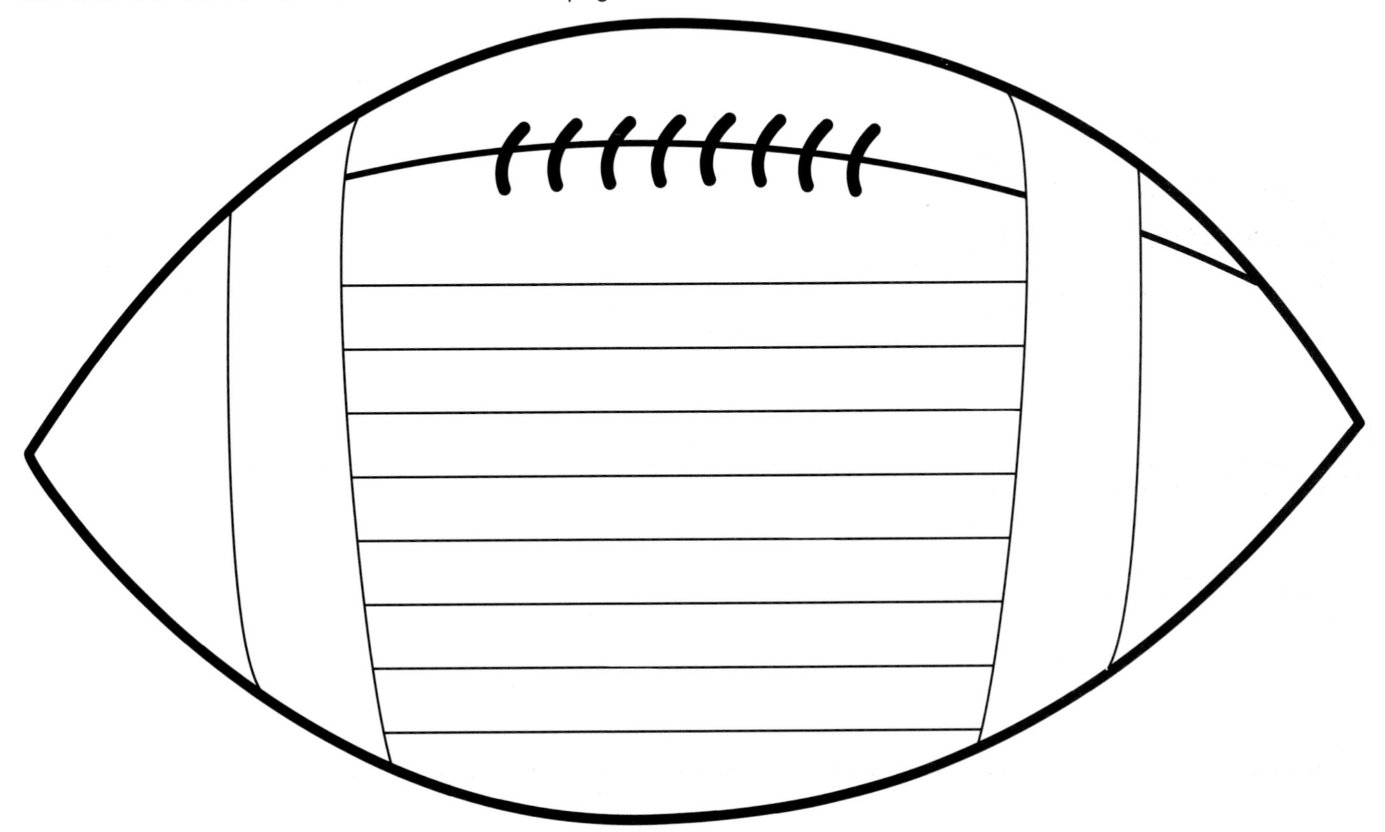

Patterns

Use with "Blast Off Into A New Year!" on page 27.

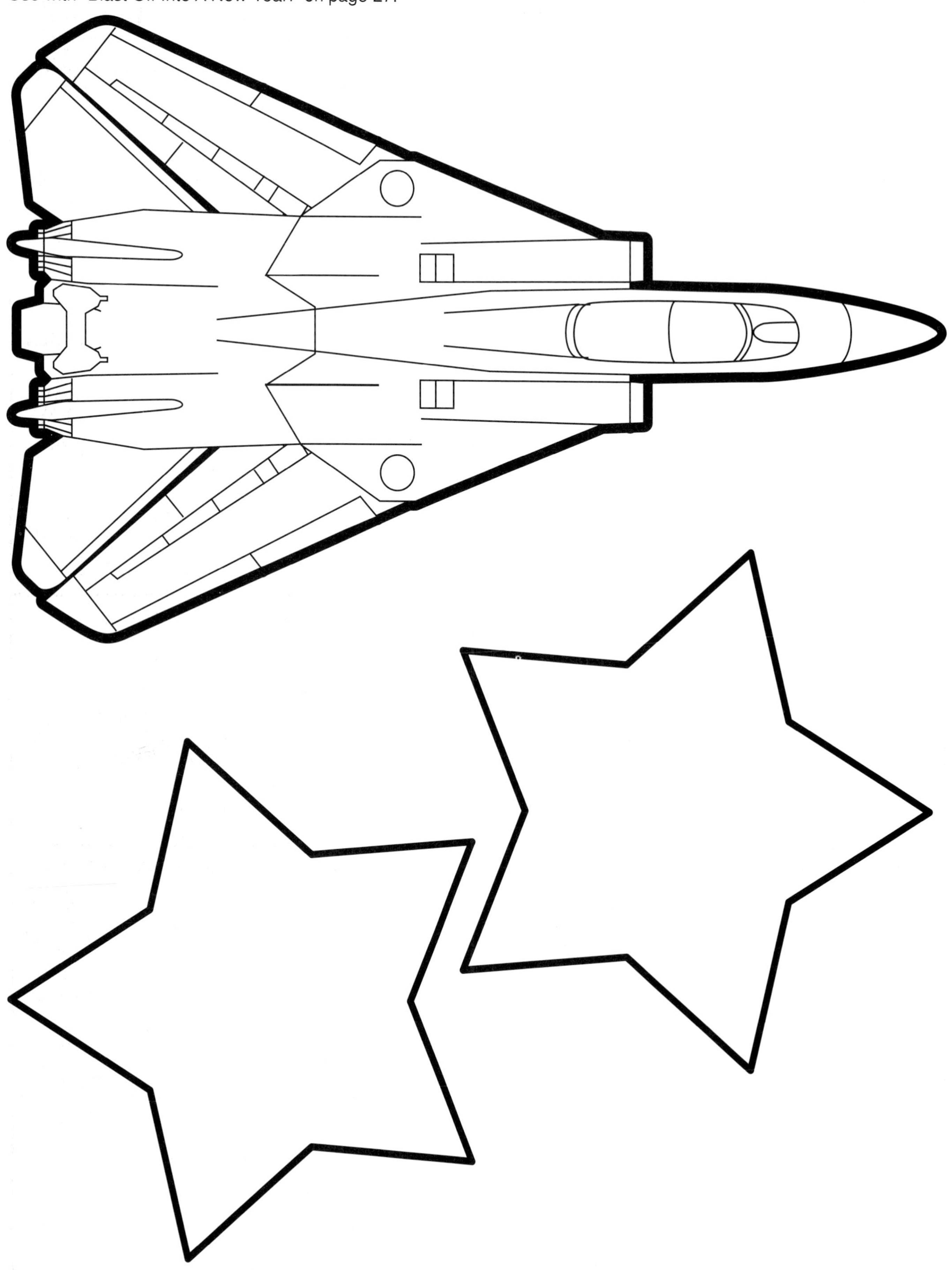

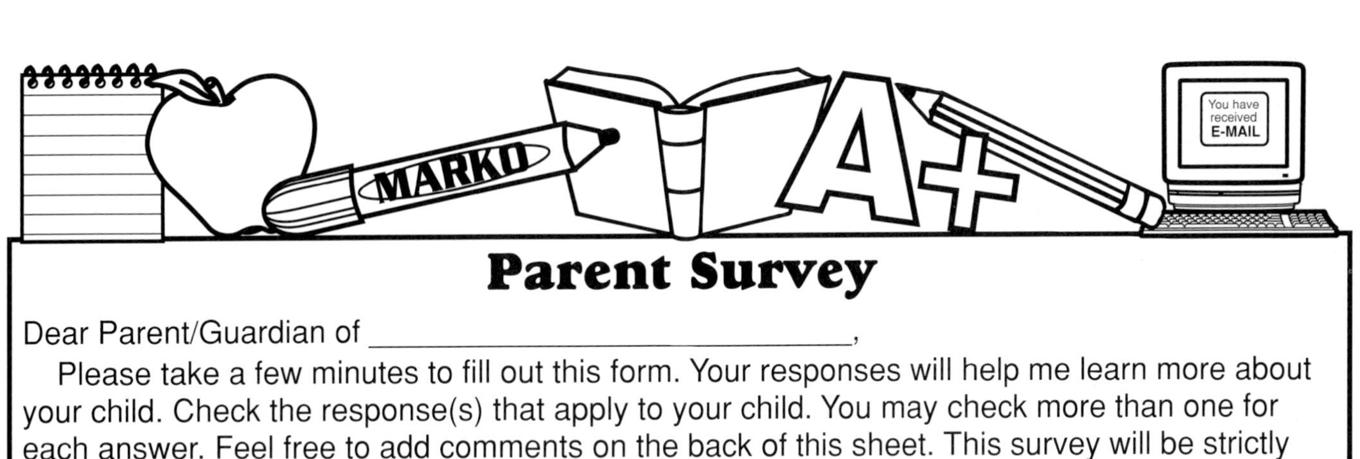

Parent Survey

Dear Parent/Guardian of ______________________________,

Please take a few minutes to fill out this form. Your responses will help me learn more about your child. Check the response(s) that apply to your child. You may check more than one for each answer. Feel free to add comments on the back of this sheet. This survey will be strictly confidential. Thank you in advance for your help!

Sincerely,

____

My child usually approaches learning...

_____ with curiosity.
_____ with confidence.
_____ with excitement.
_____ with anxiety.
_____ with reluctance.
_____ without interest.

My child learns best...

_____ by listening.
_____ by watching.
_____ by doing.

My child finds it challenging to...

_____ pay attention.
_____ follow directions.
_____ behave appropriately.
_____ speak in front of others.

My child's favorite subject(s) is (are)...

_____ math.
_____ science.
_____ social studies.
_____ reading.
_____ writing.

$E=mc^2$

My child's special talents, abilities, and interests include...

____
____
____
______________________________.

How would you describe your child's reading habits? My child...

_____ enjoys reading with others.
_____ enjoys reading alone.
_____ reads well, but is reluctant to read.
_____ does not read on his/her own.

List any other information you feel would be helpful in making this a great year for your child.

____
____
____
____

Note To The Teacher: Use this reproducible with "A Parent's Point Of View" on page 38.

Phone Call Data Sheet

Student ______________________ Home telephone ______________

Parent(s)/Guardian(s) ______________ Work telephone ______________

1. Date of phone call: ______________________________

2. Purpose of phone call: ______________________________

3. Parent/Guardian comments: ______________________________

4. Evaluation of call/Follow-up: ______________________________

Weekly Report

Student: ______________________ Date: ______________

Number of papers in this packet: ______________

Class Work

_____ Complete and on time. Great job!

_____ Late assignments:

_____ Missing assignments:

Homework

_____ Complete and on time. Great job!

_____ Late assignments:

_____ Missing assignments:

Behavior

☐ Good ☐ Fair ☐ Poor

Parent signature: ______________________________

Note To The Teacher: Use the "Phone Call Data Sheet" with "Phone Home!" on page 39. Use the "Weekly Report" with "Weekly Progress Reports" on page 41.

Star-Studded Student!

____
(Name)

____
(Date)

It's your time to shine! You're the next "Star-Studded Student" of the week! Plan on receiving some V.I.P. treatment!

Things I plan to bring in and share with my classmates:

____

____

____

Guests I plan to invite to my class include:

____

____

Things I want to tell my classmates about myself:

____

____

____

Responsibility Counts!

Name: _______________________

You have been selected to be my assistant the week of _______________.

Your responsibilities and privileges are listed below:

Responsibilities
- take lunch count
- run errands
- erase and wash the boards
- pass out and collect papers
- grade papers
- tutor students
- other: _______________

Privileges
- line leader for the week
- free "Homework Pass"
- first to get a drink and use the rest room
- first to receive classroom supplies, materials, etc.
- free prize from the "Surprise Box"
- read a favorite book to the class
- other: _______________

Note To The Teacher: Use "Star-Studded Student!" with "Shining Students" on page 46. Use "Responsibility Counts!" with "Responsibility Counts" on page 47.

Pattern

Use with "A Banner Year!" on page 47.

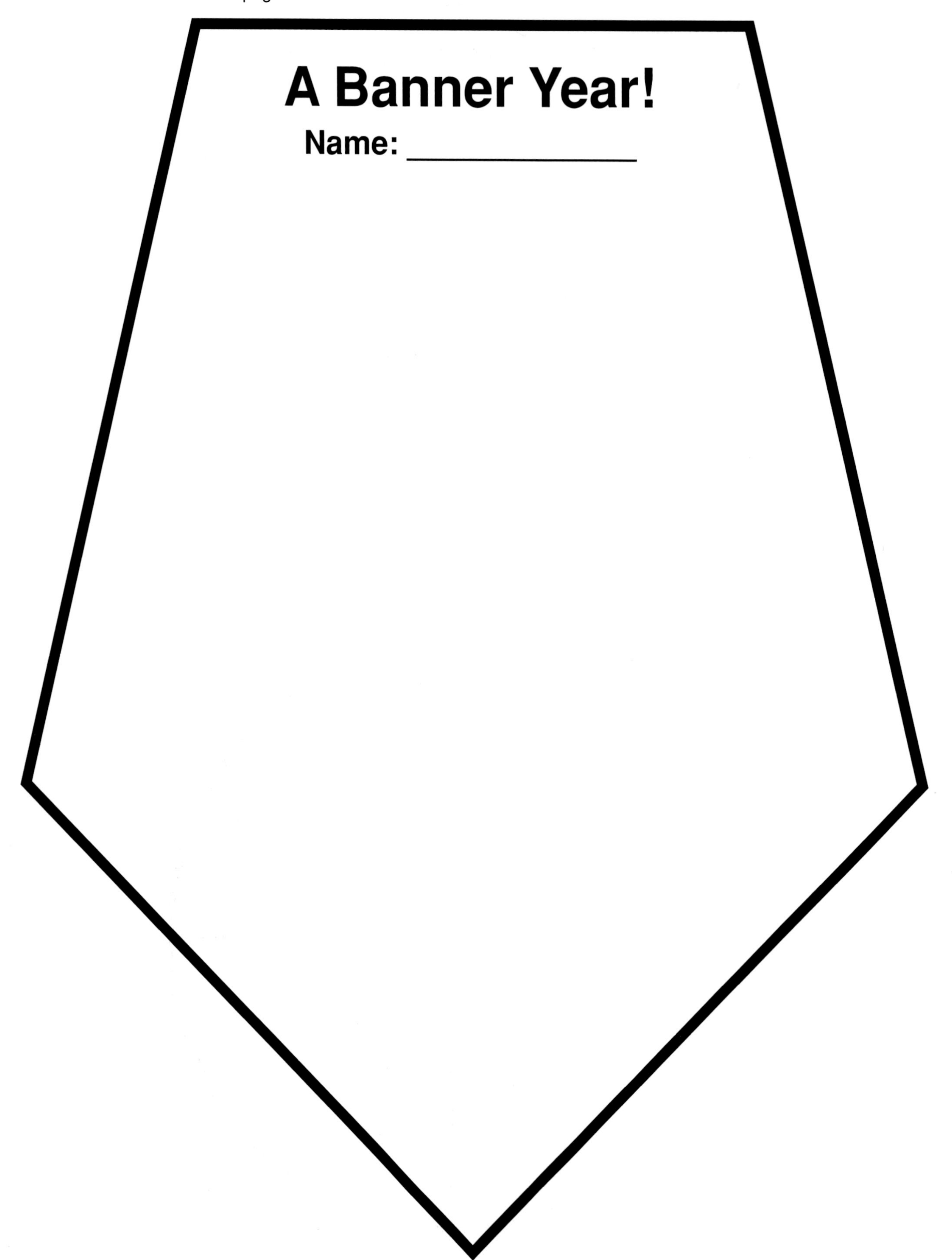

Use with "On The Road To Success" on page 52.

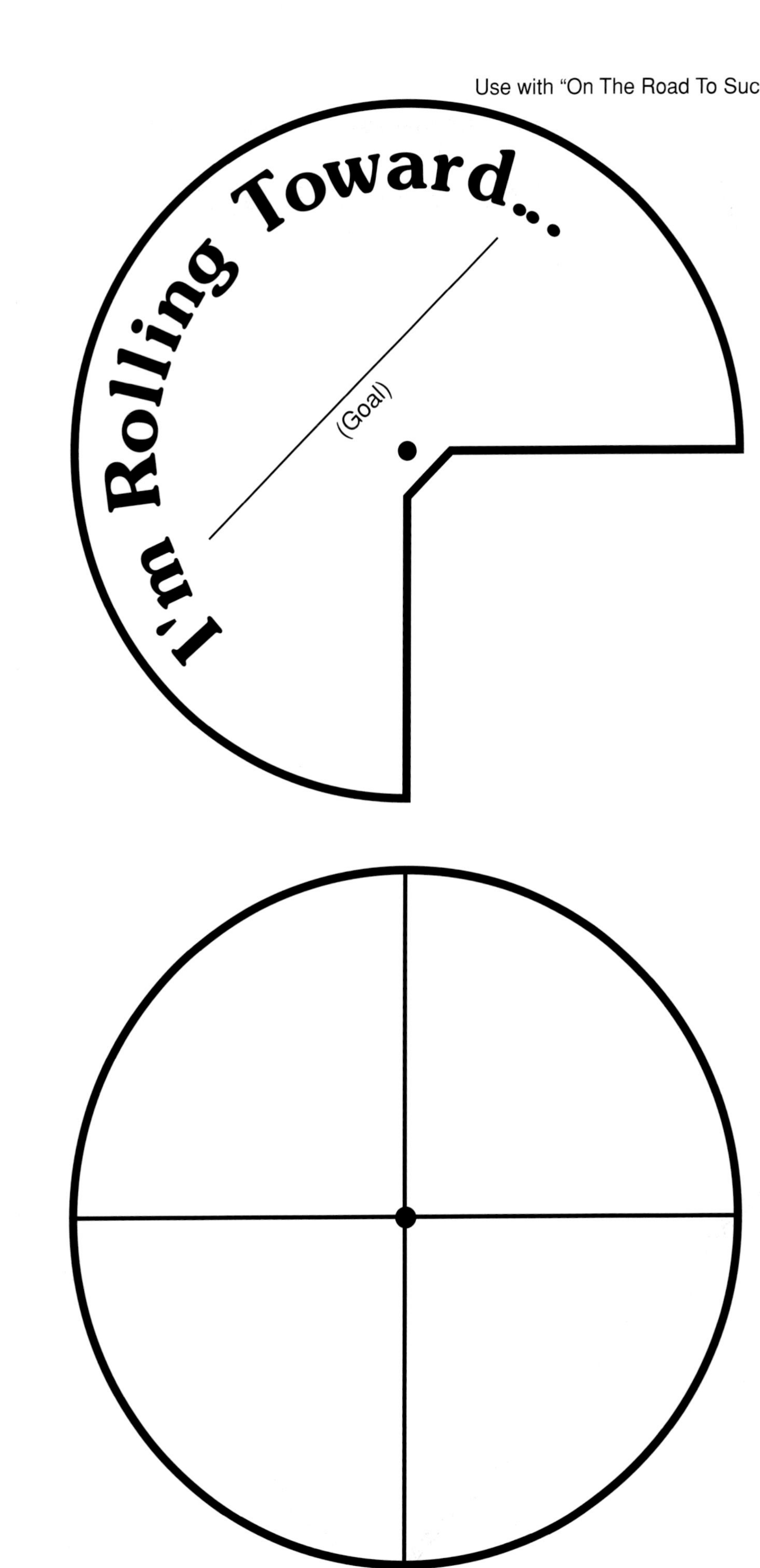

Pattern

Use with "Homework IOUs" on page 53.

Name ______________________________

Date	Assignment	Reason For Incomplete/Missing Work	Date Completed

Parent's Signature: ______________________________

Pattern

Use with "Reusable Pictograph Paper Dolls" on page 57.

Pattern

Use with "Showcase Of The Stars" on page 65.

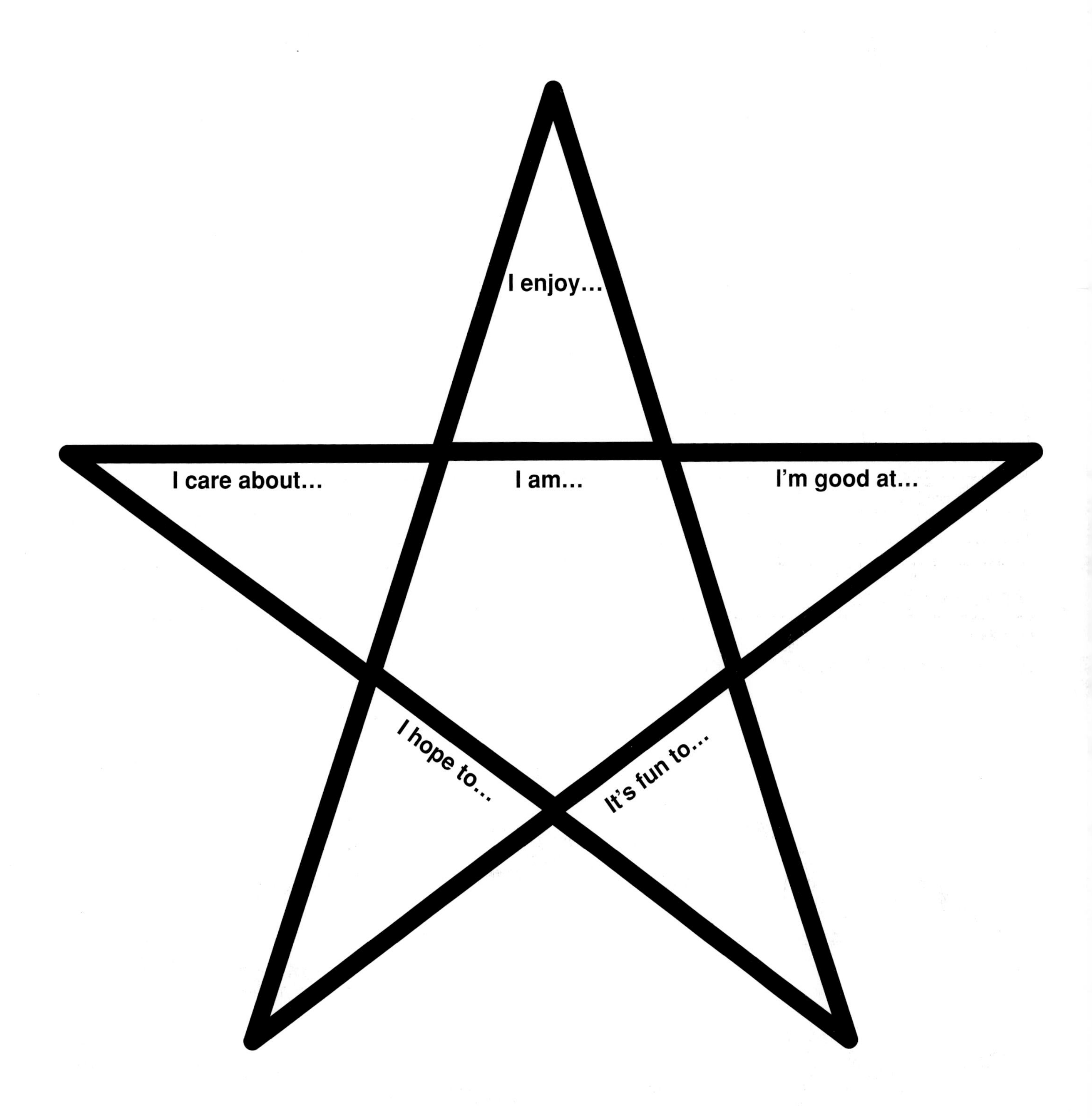

Book-Talk Map

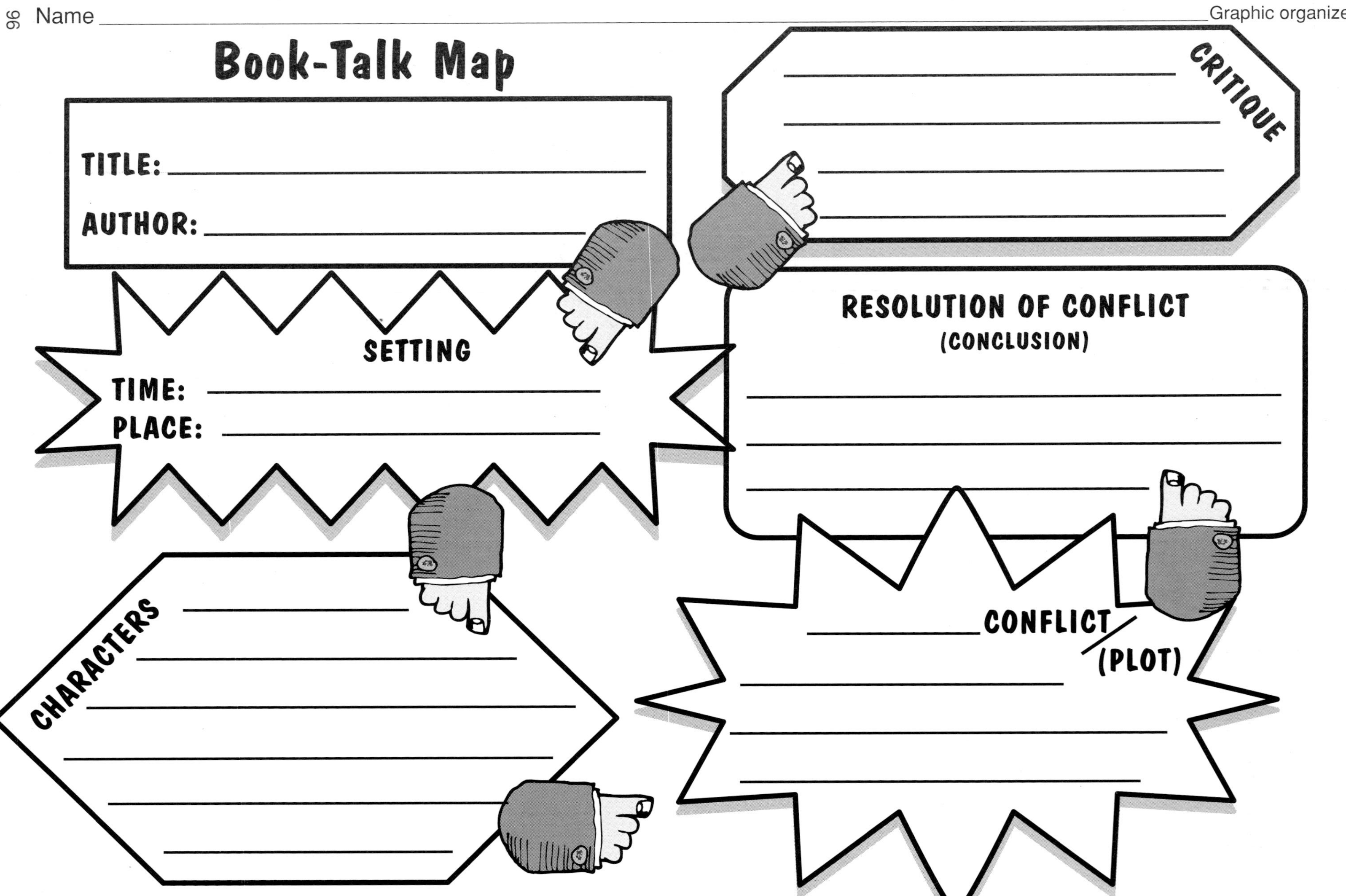

Note To The Teacher: Use with "Talking It Up!" on page 72.